SALES REV[illegible]LUTION!

[illegible]L McCOY-WARD

"This conc[illegible] Sales People - from the nuts and b[illegible]sticated closing techniques."
Paul Sloane, T[illegible] & Author of over 25 books on 'Innovation'

"Brilliant! Written by a salesperson for sales people. Neil understands the psychology behind the purchasing process and guides the reader through his uniquely designed 'Sales Revolution Model' - Actionable steps that will benefit both the novice and the skilled professional. A fantastic people centred approach for getting bigger and better sales results."
Joy Marsden, Author of 'Keep Stepping!' and Award Winning International Self-Success Speaker

"This book exposes Neil McCoy-Ward's unique three part sales success system for the very first time. As you would expect from a system developed from hard won experience of what it really takes to succeed in sales, this book contains powerful and practical principles that anyone can use to achieve superior sales results."
Simon Hazeldine: Bestselling author of "Neuro-Sell: How Neuroscience Can Power Your Sales Success" and "Bare Knuckle Selling

"Neil McCoy-Ward's new book is testament to his work in the field as both a sales professional and sales trainer. When Neil trained one of our sales teams, the results were unlike anything I had ever seen in my years of experience in this field. The performance of this team was quite literally mind blowing. This book finally reveals his secrets and opens the treasure chest for others to follow in his footsteps."
Lewis Borg, Director, Right 2 Improve Ltd (UK).

"After decades as a seasoned sales professional, sales trainer and owner of several businesses across many industries, I can honestly say that this sales book is among the best I've ever read. It's so simple to follow, refreshing to read and most importantly, easy to implement. I personally sought the mentorship from Neil McCoy-Ward as my sales trainer a few years back when I wanted to take my game to the next level. Working with Neil, I saw first hand, his unique skill and ability - it was unbelievable, and I am a Sales Trainer myself! So whether you're simply considering entering a career in sales, starting or growing your own business, or you're a hardened sales professional, this book will form an essential part of your sales kit..."
Grant Murrell, International Speaker, Sales Trainer and Radio Show Host

Sales Revolution!

First edition 2017; Revised first edition 2019

A CIP record for this title is available from the British Library.

ISBN 978-0-9957704-0-9

Typesetting and page layout by gC graphic design, Wantage.

Printed in the UK with Xpedient Print.

CONTENTS

ABOUT THE AUTHOR

Neil McCoy-Ward is the go-to expert for professionals and companies to achieve 'exceptional sales` results within a short space of time.

SALES EXPERT

Neil is a leading authority on sales training, and the World's go-to trainer for:

- **Face to face**, sales professionals (or consultants), who are required to negotiate **high-ticket** sales of products or services.
- Training of over 10,000 sales professionals and consultants around the World who use Neil's: **Sales Revolution System** ™.

KEYNOTE SPEAKER

Neil has been a professional keynote speaker since 2008, having delivered over 1,000 speeches to people across 5 continents.

ENTREPRENEUR

Neil walks the talk and personally owns businesses that span many sectors including: Real Estate, Property Lettings/ Management, Home Improvements, Hospitality, Event Management, Retail, Training for Schools/Universities, Marketing Training, Sales Training, Keynote Speaking, Business & Personal Mentoring and more. All of his companies follow this **Sales Revolution System** ™.

MILITARY

Neil served in the British Army for over 10 years, 3 of those years with the British Special Forces and retired as a Sergeant.

PREFACE

Congratulations for choosing to skyrocket your sales results by purchasing this book and taking the action herein. This sales system (yes, this is a system, not just a boring sales book) WILL completely change your life, just as it has done for over 10,000+ people currently using the Sales Revolution System ™ around the World. This system, is now the most widely used sales system for big-ticket, face to face sales in the World.

Once you understand the system and start to implement it, you really can go from the worst salesperson in the company, to the very top in a matter of months; outperforming even the top sales professionals...

Let me first explain who this book is for, and who this book is not for:

Who this book is FOR:

- Sales Professionals, Sales Consultants, Sales Managers, Sales Directors; anyone required to sell products as part of your job or role
- You sell HIGH ticket products or services
- You sell face to face with your clients

Who this book is NOT for:

- Telesales professionals
- You sell LOW ticket products or services (less than £1,000/$1,000)
- You don't sell face to face, you sell via email, websites or over the phone

★★★★★

If you fit in to the latter category, you will still gain IMMENSE golden nuggets from this book, but I want to make it clear from the outset who this book is aimed at and who will get the most benefit from the system.

THE END OF SALES TRAINING AS YOU KNOW IT

A few years back, I was speaking at a national sales conference and I did the unthinkable. I disagreed with the half dozen or so sales and marketing trainers speaking at the conference on the direction that sales success would go in the next decade.

You see, the sales training industry is pretty 'old hat` – most of the trainers in the spotlight have been there since dinosaurs roamed the earth. They are not there by pure skill and excellence, but simply by TIME.

The problem with TIME is that as it goes by, things change. Sales trainers and the techniques they teach, unfortunately in the most part – have not.

This is why in the last century, nearly all of the books published on 'Sales' in the marketplace teach the same principles. It's rare that you pick up a book and discover some new sales techniques or system, geared towards the modern World.

This is the promise of this book: using cutting edge, real time strategies that have been used in the field, by hundreds of my own sales professionals through thousands of presentations/pitches to prospects all over the Western World – we know what works (and we CRUSH it, by the way).

This book is going to teach you my EXACT system for how I achieved a 1:1.2 sales ratio in the big-ticket product sales industry, selling face to face to customers all on the same day. This was unheard of in an industry where a good sales ratio was 1:3 (1 sale per 3 appointments) Vs my ratio of 1 sale in 1.2 appointments, or put more simply, (4 sales out of every 5 appointments), all from same day cold calls to signed contracts face to face for 5 figures.

Now if I were selling widgets costing the same as a cup of coffee, this would not be a great achievement, but I wasn't, I was selling systems that started at £6,000 and went up to £12,000. My commission on these systems was 10%. Sales can be a very lucrative business to be in once you understand this system.

In a 12-month period, I personally sold over £1.2m of product; this didn't include the sales of my team for whom I got a 1% cut on everything they sold throughout the UK. This is how you get wealthy from being in sales.

The other way is to sell higher end products or services, because the more the item costs, the higher the payout on your commissions:

e.g a 5% commission would pay out:
5% on £100 = £5
5% on £1,000 = £50
5% on £10,000 = £500
5% on £100,000 = £5,000

5% on £1,000,000 = £50,000
You get the idea…

The challenge: the bigger a company gets, the bigger the problems they face, and the more reliance they have on making and increasing their sales.

As a sales professional, if you can solve these problems by selling more product for yourself or for your company, your family will never go hungry and you can get extremely rich… (if that's your goal).

The other challenge is that the company is more likely to do one of two things:

One: they will call in some high end firm of 'consultants' to solve the problem, when they really need someone like me, or someone like you, the sales people already within the organisation to solve the challenge.

Or Two: They ask the sales manager to step into the shoes of a sales trainer, which can also be a disaster if it's the sales manager that's currently causing the low sales or problems to begin with!

The final challenge is when a company is paying a sales manager or trainer a **salary** as opposed to the pay being **performance based**. It's been proven through countless studies that these are the worst performing sales roles as salarised salespeople have no incentive to increase company sales because they get paid no matter what.

BRIDGING THE GAP

The challenge when initially writing this book was that I had to collect all my knowledge and research on Evolutionary Biology & Psychology, Neuroscience, Neuro Linguistic Programming, and other Sciences – all complex topics, and make them into a simple to understand system that anyone could follow.

I feel I've achieved this by creating a simple 3 PART system. It clearly tells you WHAT to do, without going to deep into the science behind it. A friend of mine said to me one day, "Neil, I couldn't care less how my TV works… I just want to know how to use the remote." With this in mind, I'm going to cover 3 parts:

1. Market
2. Solution
3. Offer

Which is broken down further into 9 segments as seen in the image on the next page:

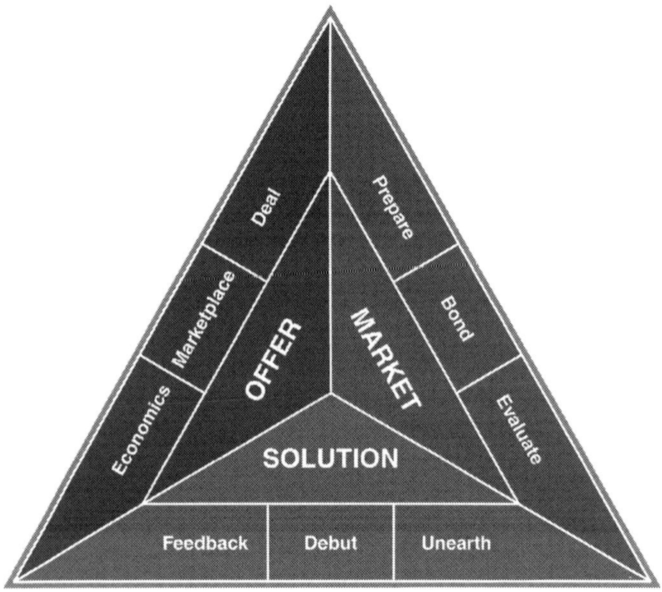

Sales Revolution System™

Market:

1. Prepare
2. Bond
3. Evaluate

Solution:

1. Unearth
2. Debut
3. Feedback

Offer:

1. Economics
2. Marketplace
3. Deal

INTRODUCTION

Many people often ask me about my journey in the World of sales and how I went from entry level (knowing less than nothing) to being one of the top sales trainers in the World within 3 years...

I had a massive advantage over most people, for two reasons.

One: I worked with British Special Forces for three years out of my ten year Army career, and learned skills that made me view people and how they make decisions in a whole new light. Added to the fact that my mindset was different to other salespeople who I met. If times got hard in my line of work in the military, I didn't have the option of going home to watch TV or having an ice cold beer... I had to just figure it out, find a way to achieve the objective, no matter what.

Two: I worked for one of the top marketing consultants in the World in California for a year before going into sales: marketing and sales tend to go hand in hand so I guess you could say I had a World class mentor in that respect.

But even with all that experience, if you have a bad sales mentor, you're done for. Unfortunately for me, I had the worst. A man that couldn't sell anything himself, so the management made him a trainer – great logic there!

My first sales role was a disaster, I was terrible... I sold nothing for a long time and had to borrow money from my Dad to keep me afloat. My finances were so bad that I went from driving a new car to driving a £500 VW Polo Boulevard that only had 4 gears with a max speed of 60mph and resembled a metal box on wheels.

For every sales appointment, I parked five minutes walk away from wherever I was going. I ate in McDonalds every day for lunch and dinner as that's all I could afford and I rented a tiny room in a shared house for £300.00 a month. Life sucked. How had I gone from an amazing Army career where I had everything I ever wanted, to THIS… My initial thought was to track down the guy who advised me to go into sales…

This unfortunately is the cold reality of being in sales in your first few months, especially if you are in direct sales and earn commission only with no base salary. Although it's massively frowned upon, it's actually very common in most direct sales roles to have no base salary.

After a few months, I got it, I figured out how to sell my product – and sell it I did! Once you 'get it` as a salesperson, you become an unstoppable force; it's addictive. The more sales you make, the more drive and motivation you get, especially when you see the money for the first time and it just keeps rolling in...

I became so skilled at sales that after the first twelve months, I built my own sales team, who I had taken from having no sales experience, to being 'exceptional' sales professionals. Our team became so good in fact, that just three of us, were outselling every other team throughout the syndicate of companies. Even though the others had more salespeople, resources, marketing and client databases.

Other sales people started to approach me to ask for help and the more I showed people what I was doing, the more their sales and conversion rates went up too. Soon my company was selling so much product, that we were outselling all the other companies in the syndicate combined.

Three months later I was asked to work for a sister sales company as the National sales trainer for their big-ticket products. Each week, salespeople from around the UK would drive up to 10 hours for a two-hour training session with me.

After two years I had reached the level where I was not only training sales managers and directors, but I was now training top level sales teams all over the World.

The question that most people have on their minds at this point when they hear my story is: How did you do it?! How did you sell over £1.2M of products within the space of just twelve months, and get to train world-class sales teams in this sales technique? How did you go from newbie to sales training expert within just two years?

Here is the answer... By using the 'exact' system you're going to learn in this book.

★★★★★

The Sales Revolution System, did not come about by accident. It was the result of thousands of hours of research, testing, implementing and tweaking until I was 100% happy that the system could work for anyone, in any industry, under any circumstances. Added to this, reading 50+ other sales books, being mentored by world-class sales trainers, constantly teaching the system to the other people in my team, and finally touring and teaching the system to other direct sales companies. Out of this, the Sales Revolution System was not only born, but MASTERED.

Sales is one of the most rewarding professions in the world, if you can master this art, your income as a sales professional will be uncapped. You will reach the position that so many other students who I've trained have, where you can write your own paycheck and demand any price you desire for your unique skill set.

Being able to sell well really is a unique skill set. A brain surgeon may have a unique skill set which pays him or her a very large sum of money, and you may consider them extremely wealthy. However, even a brain surgeon cannot compete with the salary of a leading sales professional who is able to sell hundreds, or even thousands of big-ticket items each year.

One sales professional that came to one of my trainings had started as a failing car salesman working at a local garage, and earned less than £15,000 a year. Within 18 months, this man had gone from local garage, to selling supercars earning in excess of £180,000 in commissions. This is the power of the sales profession; you really can be, and earn whatever you want for your life, if you just CHOOSE to.

★★★★★

> **The difficulty is and always has been staying motivated against adversity.**

You will hit roadblocks all the way, you will hit rejection, you will have people being rude to you, you will have people telling you you're not good enough, you will have people trying to stop you, and trying to sabotage you from achieving your goals and dreams.

What really makes a difference, is whether you will get up after each knock down and keep on moving forward no matter what. Because most people just won't do that; they will get knocked down and they won't get up again, they won't take the hits that are required to reach success and this is why so many people get to the end of their life, look back, and have regrets. Don't be one of those people, don't be that person 80 years old in the hospital bed looking back on your life with regrets. This is your chance, this is your opportunity right now to make a difference in your life, not just for yourself, but for your family and friends too.

....

Finally, before we start the course content, I'm going to make one and only one sales 'plug' to you, simply because this book is all about YOU, and getting you to earn more, so I don't want to follow the parasitic trend emerging with authors who fill their books with 90% promotion and 10% content, this book will be 99% content and this 1% plug…

On my website: neilmccoyward.com, I offer several services that I hope you will bookmark now, including:

- Keynote Speeches (for Conferences)
- Corporate Training (I will come to your workplace and

train your teams)
- Personal Mentoring (If you feel that you would like to have someone hold you accountable and guide you towards the top 1%, you can join my annual mentoring program – numbers extremely limited)

Please check these services out, I guarantee you will not regret it. Over 10,000 sales professionals around the World can't be wrong…

That's it, plug over. Enjoy your course and the wealth it will bring you…

Neil McCoy-Ward,

CHAPTER 1

SECTION I: MARKET

SUB SECTION I: PREPARE

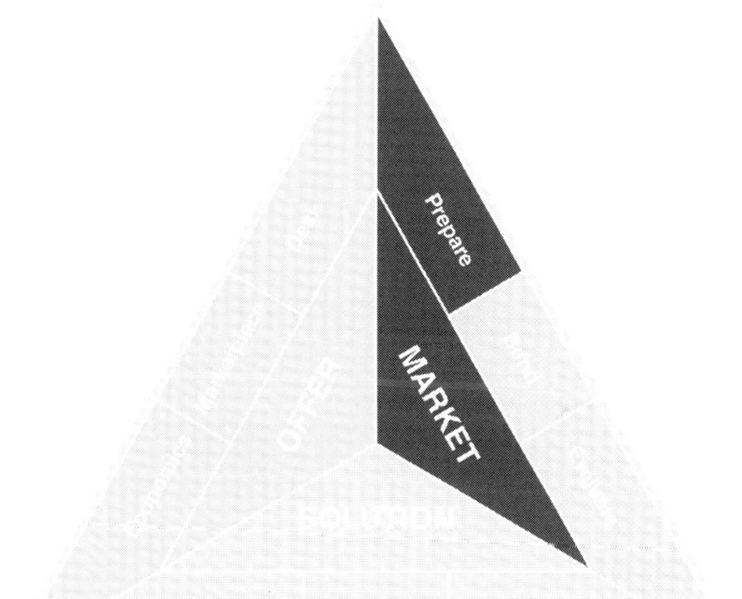

Sales Revolution System™

Stage 1 is about planning and preparation, which is the most IMPORTANT step in the entire process, and yet this is the step that most sales professionals pay the least attention and effort to.

Why is this step so important and why is it placed at the Number one position?

Let's compare this step to building a house... Whether you want to build the house yourself or you want to hire a home builder to build for you, think about how you would go about it right now.

Would you tell the builder to just go for it and build whatever he wants? Highly unlikely. What you would probably do is to view lots of different houses, go to many trade shows, consult with an architect, interview various builders and after all this is done, you would start looking for a plot of land and then get quotes for the cost of the build. Once you have all this, you would then get your architect to create drawings and designs. Only once all of this has been completed, would you even consider starting the build.

Now take the above example, and apply this to a sales appointment. Would you ever go to an appointment not properly prepared? Common sense would say no, but yet over 80% of sales professionals do so without any prior planning or preparation. Acting in this way will almost certainly result in failure, or reduced efficiency over the long-term for your income and success.

My role throughout this book as I see it, is to make you a more effective sales professional. Effectiveness in sales consists of many factors, one of which is being efficient in time and energy. I still remember an appointment where my (very bad) mentor and I, had driven over two hours to visit a gentleman who wanted to save money on his heating bill. This gentleman had a large country estate, was very wealthy and we had the exact product that would 'solve his problem.'

Upon arriving at what we believed was the appointment address; I noticed that there was nothing but old barns and livestock for miles around. Being new to sales and in my first week, I said nothing and assumed my mentor knew something I didn't. He then started to get very flustered and started driving around holding his phone up in the air attempting to get a signal. He was getting more and more frustrated by the minute as we were now over 20 minutes late and his face was as red as a beetroot.

By the time we arrived at the appointment, we were over one hour late and the gentleman only had 45 minutes left before his next appointment. He was very disappointed that we had not maintained our integrity and arrived on time, which made me feel terrible as I really prize my timekeeping and felt powerless, as I was not in control.

Needless to say that this gentleman homeowner never became a customer of my mentor, but nine months later, I went back to that estate and sold him £17,000 worth of renewable heating systems, earning me a £1,700 (10%) commission for a few hours' worth of work.

What were the mistakes that my mentor had made?

- Always check the address on the map and confirm the location with the customer by phone.
- Always plan to arrive a minimum of 15 minutes prior to the appointment, 30 minutes for more important

appointments, especially if you must travel a considerable distance.

- If driving to your appointment, invest in a back-up satellite navigation system (sat nav) for your car and ensure the maps are updated regularly. However, Google Maps is my preferred choice. Of course, you will also need an 'in-car charger' as navigating using your phone really does deplete your battery quickly.
- Remain calm and don't lose your cool or this ruins your positive state of mind and a positive attitude is more important than anything else.
- If you arrive late, apologise profusely and don't pretend that you were 'supposed' to arrive at this time making the customer wrong.
- Don't blame other people back at the office for not giving you clear directions; it is your responsibility to check before setting out.
- Don't ever talk badly about the customer stating: "they were a bad lead".

You may think that I didn't learn anything from my mentor, but on the contrary, I learned more from him than I did from most others after him. Why? Because he taught me all the things not to do as a sales professional! The admiration in my eyes, soon turned to pity when I saw how he took no responsibility for his failings and even worse, made other people feel bad who were supporting us back at the office by blaming them for his shortcomings. Although he was considered wealthy due to his income, his health and personal life were suffering quite badly, this is where balance comes in which we will discuss later. Also remember that no sales professional ever acts alone, you are part of one big cohesive team, from your lead makers right through to your distribution channel.

Your Action Steps prior to any appointment:

- **KNOW who your competitors are – know everything about their product or service and their price point, the more knowledge you have, the more POWER you have**
- Ensure your appointment has been confirmed with the client
- Check that you have the correct address
- Research your customer and understand their current problems or challenges
- Ensure you have identification (ID) on you
- Ensure your car is clean and presentable
- Ensure your phone is fully charged
- Pack brochures and literature
- Pack all relevant paperwork needed, including contracts
- A well-presented bag/briefcase
- Ensure your own appearance is as expected for the level of appointment
- If the appointment is at your office, ensure it has been cleaned before your client arrives
- The office seating must be comfortable and clean
- Have someone provide your client with refreshments

CONFIRMING THE APPOINTMENT

If you are part of a professional sales company, you will no doubt have your own 'confirmer' in the office, or at least your team will have a 'confirmer'. The confirmer will often be the sales manager in some companies. Although it is their responsibility to confirm each appointment before sending you out, if you find your manager incompetent, I would recommend you take this task away from them so you can always double check the information yourself before setting off. This is a win-win as you will sell more by wasting less time, and your sales manager will have less work to do.

★★★★★

There is nothing worse than commuting two or three hours only to arrive at the appointment to find that it was not confirmed correctly and you are unable to have the appointment. It's a long commute back to the office or home I can assure you!

If you work on your own and it's your responsibility to confirm each appointment, I would recommend calling the customer prior to the appointment, whether you are traveling to them, or if they are coming to you, you should always confirm again on the day of the appointment.

Many sales trainers will tell you <u>NOT</u> to call the customer. Their reason for saying not to re-confirm the appointment, is because the customers sometimes change their mind overnight, especially if the lead has come from a cold call. I completely disagree, because from my experience, those customers probably didn't want the appointment in the first place and often cancel on you when you arrive or will conveniently 'be out'.

The best appointment is where your customer has a very real need and problem that requires a solution, if that's the case and they have nothing to lose, why would they even consider canceling an appointment? Again, I go back to my reasoning that the only appointments that cancel under these circumstances are where the customer didn't really want the appointment in the first place, and it has been almost forced upon them by one of the telephone marketing team, this is more common than you would think.

Always re-confirm the appointment, this will save you not only lots of time in canceled or unworkable appointments, but a lot of peace of mind and mental energy which you can apply to prospecting or serving your current customer base.

★★★★★

CORRECT ADDRESS

I've never understood why the majority of sales professionals don't check the address on a map before setting out on their appointment; this makes no sense to me whatsoever. Once you've confirmed the correct address with your customer, I would recommend that you open up 'Google Maps' (this is the most accurate map service as of writing.) Type the address into the search bar and confirm the location with the address you have from your customer. Once you see that the address matches the map, you should now plot the route from the location you will be setting out from. This is an important step because our brain always <u>underestimates</u> the time it will take to make the journey, this is why people are so often late for work or meetings.

If you are based in a city, particularly a large city, I would also recommend using the 'arrive/depart' function within Google Maps as it allows you to plot your journey by day and time, this will account for morning and evening rush hour which you may not get in smaller cities, towns or villages. I discovered this problem whilst riding with my mentor, where he would never allow for morning or evening rush hour traffic and we would arrive late at our appointments every time!

RESEARCH YOUR CUSTOMER

Who is your customer? Are they the decision-maker or the gatekeeper? How old are they? Why do they need your product or service? What are their current challenges? How can you solve their problems? What can you offer that is above and beyond what they currently have? Have they bought a similar product before? And if so how much did they spend? What is their budget?

I could list a hundred more questions like this that you should be asking yourself about your customer to assess their buying patterns. When you have this information, you are in a great position.

Another thing the majority of salespeople don't do, is they just don't go through this process of finding out who the customer really is and most importantly what the problems are, and if you can solve those problems.

Let's take an example: pretend you are in the middle of the desert dying of dehydration and someone offers you a glass of water for a reasonable price. Would you buy that glass of water? Of course you would! There isn't a single person on the planet that would NOT buy that class of water in order to save their own life.

Sales success is really just about applying good common sense and solving people's problems. Sales success isn't about trying to sell products or services to people who don't really 'want' them. Often times I see salespeople trying to sell products to customers who just don't want or need their product.

Going back to the dehydration example, it would be like offering the person dying of thirst… a bucket of sand! That person will never buy a bucket of sand from you, no matter how low your price, how many special sand related bonuses you give them, or how many years interest free credit is available. They don't need a bucket of sand right now, they need a bucket of water. If people don't have a need or desire for your product or service, it's very unlikely that you will ever become successful selling it.

At this point it's worth contemplating and considering the

product range that you currently sell to the open market. Do you believe in your products/services? Or are there better products/services out there that make your products look second place?

Please don't get me wrong, there is a clear distinction between **needs** and **wants** which we will cover later on.

People are far more likely to purchase a **want** than they are a **need**, again this is counter intuitive to logic and common sense. Why do people buy one Ferrari when they can buy TEN brand new Ford vehicles for the same price? Why do people buy a huge twenty-bedroom mansion house for a family of four when a four-bedroom home would suffice? Why do people buy a Rolex for £10,000 when they could purchase a good quality Swiss watch for £100?

It all comes down to wants and not needs. People make buying decisions based on emotion and they then look for ways to justify those decisions with logic, even if those reasons make no logical sense to you or I. If you can remember this point, you'll make a fortune. In fact, highlight this paragraph and even write it on your wall if need be.

Welcome to the World of the 'irrational' human being.

ALWAYS CARRY IDENTIFICATION

If you are visiting customers' homes & offices, I highly recommend that you ask your company to create an identification card for you. The homeowner will feel more comfortable seeing photographic identification with your name and company on it. If you work in a business-to-business role, a photo ID card will be absolutely necessary in most cases due to security.

★★★★★

ENSURE YOUR CAR IS CLEAN AND FUELED

We now come on to the age-old argument, just how important is it to have a nice car when attending a sales appointment? Having been asked this question hundreds of times now I think I've finally got the answer.

If you work in a business-to-business sales environment, the more luxurious your car, the better.

If you work in direct sales, and you visit homeowners at their home, you want to drive an average car. Not too expensive and not to cheap. A good reliable family car works best.

And here's the psychology behind it…

Successful businesses like to work with other successful businesses. If you turn up for a B2B (Business to Business) sales meeting in a cheap car, and you ask for a high-value order, it will instantly feel 'off' to the customer, it just won't feel right. Your customer won't be able to put their finger on it as to why it doesn't feel right to go ahead, but their subconscious mind will know the reason. Again it comes down to congruency, or in this case in-congruency. It is not congruent to turn up for a business meeting in a cheap car, and to then ask for a high order. The brain asks itself: if you're really worth this high price point, why are you driving such a low priced car? It doesn't make sense, something's wrong here. If I drive a low cost car as a leading sales trainer, I can assure you that I would not be seen in the same light. This is why I drive a luxury car.

Let's flip this now then:

When visiting homeowners, if you turn up in a luxurious

car, the homeowner instantly thinks: "this is going to cost a lot of money" or "he/she must earn huge commissions to be able to pay for a car like that." You don't want your customer to think either of these things! If they think that what you're offering is going to cost a huge sum of money, they will lie to you, give you incorrect information, and have their guard up all the way through the appointment, even if you have exactly what they are looking for. That's if they don't come up with a reason for you to not enter their home in the first place.

Also, if they think that you are going to rip them off, or that you make huge commissions from the sale, again, they may not want to purchase because they don't want their money to go on your car and lifestyle. This is why it's important when visiting your customers at home, to drive a regular family car. This portrays you as the nice family man/lady next door, and this is who homeowners prefer to deal with. I can say this with confidence as I made just as few sales when driving my crappy £500 car as I did driving a luxury car. When I hit big was when I switched to an everyday family car.

I still remember the day when my mentor took me out for the day on some appointments in his brand new luxury car. He was very proud of this car having just spent £50,000 CASH on it brand new from the dealership. The first appointment of the day was a pretty tough one, all the way through the appointment the man was suspicious of my mentor claiming to be just a simple engineer, and yet he was driving a luxury vehicle. By the time he got to the order form, the customer was adamant that he wanted a better price and he kept mentioning my mentor's luxury car parked outside. Then the customer said these exact words: "I'm not paying you

£8,000, because I bet £1,000 of my money goes to funding that car! I'll pay you £6,000 and not a penny more!" My mentor accepted the price and made a small £200 commission on the sale, instead of £800 (10%).

Note: in most sales companies, there will be a sliding scale for commissions, 10% will be paid for a full price sale dropping down as low as 2% for a low priced sale of the same item.

I heard years later that he finally took my advice and now either parks his car a few minutes' walk away or drives his girlfriend's car instead and his sales have increased.

The next important point is to ensure that your car is always full of fuel. I would make it a rule, that if upon the end of a workday your tank had less than half of fuel left, to fill it up right away before retiring for the night. Never start any day with less than half the fuel in your tank, no matter how tired you are, you must have the discipline to do what needs to be done. It only takes one long sales appointment to the middle of nowhere with no fueling station around to ruin your day. I always fill my tank each evening regardless if I am at 50% or less.

When visiting your customer, you should always ensure that your car is clean and tidy. There is nothing worse than when your customer meets you at your car on arrival and it's full of dirty sports kit, old fast food wrappers, empty soda cans and bottles and of course... the smell to go with it all. You only get one chance to make a good first impression, don't ruin it by having a dirty car, both on the inside and out.

My sales team members had to get their car cleaned inside and out every weekend before our Monday morning meeting. If any of my sales people turned up for the meeting and had not cleaned their car, they would be sent away to get it cleaned before I would issue them with any appointments for the week and they would be penalised. There's just no excuse for turning up unprepared and this is why my sales teams are always Number 1.

Clean Car, Clean Mind = Ready for Success.

CHARGING YOUR PHONE

Another problem that I would often come across with my salespeople, is that occasionally towards the end of the day, I just couldn't get hold of any of them. I would often think that maybe they were just in a signal black spot or that they had gone home early for the day. But when I wouldn't get a phone call from them at the end of their appointment, I would become worried for their well-being. After several false alarms of sending out a search party to the customer's home or office location, it became apparent that we had an issue with phones running out of battery. In this line of work we make a lot of calls and use a lot of battery.

For this very reason, I implemented a new policy that all salespeople must have an 'in car phone charging' system, and external power bank and that their phone must be plugged in whilst driving between appointments. Thanks to this new policy not only did business and sales go up, but my anxiety level went down. All my sales people had to check in with me or the office at the beginning and end of each appointment, which ensured that my teams were all safe.

For your own personal safety, I would implement a system whereby you message a 'buddy' or your sales manager before and after each appointment if you are alone and it's an 'off location' appointment, especially if you're female. Now, I'm not saying that women can't handle themselves, believe me, I've met plenty of women in the Army who could take me down!

What I'm saying is that it's much more likely that women are targeted over men, and that's unacceptable to me. So if you're a sales manager, it's your duty to put a safety system in place as well as to issue your reps with a panic alarm, also known as a personal protection alarm and whatever else you deem appropriate. But again, like any challenge, let the reps on the ground come up with the solution for you, they'll do a much better job.

In my early days of sales, I had many nerve racking experiences when visiting homeowners where I was worried that I'd never get out of the house again. There are some strange and scary people out there in the world and often times you don't realise this until you're sat in their home or office with no means of escape.

The other important point with your phone, is to ensure that you have a good all-inclusive service plan. Most phone service providers will compete for your business, so it pays to shop around. Ensure you have enough minutes and data for your role as a sales professional. If your package isn't sufficient enough, you may end up paying three or four times the cost of simply upgrading to a higher package. It often pays to take out a larger phone package with excess minutes, messages and data.

BROCHURES AND LITERATURE

It always amazes me when companies spend huge sums of money on marketing, advertising and expensive offices and cars, but yet forget to make sure their paperwork and brochures are also to a high standard.

I was consulting for a company who a year previously, had received sales training from me. This company was impressive, their parking lot was full of expensive luxury cars and supercars including a Rolls Royce, Ferrari and Lamborghini. Their office was made completely of glass with polished chrome fixtures and fittings all around, it was an impressive sight. Their challenge now after boosting their sales by 70% in the past year was that they were losing a lot of business once the sales rep left the customer and they couldn't understand why.

Having spoken with the Directors at length, I was also struggling to find the reason. Everything seemed perfect, the staff were well groomed, well fitted suits, the waiting area was impressive, even the receptionist was playing the part and offered me refreshments as soon as I walked through the door. Their sales staff were well prepared, courteous, found the problems well, and solved the needs of their customers… they were playing the game very well indeed.

Because I was struggling to find the reason for all these cancellations, I was close to giving up, it just didn't make sense. Then I did what we do in the Army… when you get stuck, go back to basics: I had to then put myself into the customer's shoes in order to get into the customers head. I instructed the sales manager to take me through the process (that I had taught them a year earlier) and it went perfectly.

I was still struggling to find the reason for their cancellations as they were doing everything I had taught them. I was convinced that they were either missing a key component to the system, or they were trying to 'hard close` the customer instead of using my soft closing methods which have an incredible success rate.

However I was wrong on all counts. When we finally got to the contract and paperwork, it was clear to me what was going on. The company were selling luxury products, mainly in the form of vacations, such as private island getaways. But yet their brochures and paperwork said the complete opposite of luxury; to me their paperwork said cheap, average, the sort of brochure I would get if buying a secondhand printer for the office. A luxury brand should have a luxury brochure, not a badly designed, thrown together brochure printed on cheap card.

Of course when the husband or wife took this booking brochure to their partner, who had not sat through the presentation and seen the well-groomed, nicely dressed salesperson, you can imagine what their partner had to say. It was no surprise to learn that 90% of the cancellations were indeed from a single partner appointment. The lesson here is that everything you do has to be congruent.

I asked the head of sales why they had gotten rid of the original brochures that I, alongside a branding expert had helped them to produce. They said that they had hired a consultant psychologist to look at their business systems, and she felt that the brochures were too extravagant and over the top for their demographic of client.

This actually couldn't be further from the truth. The more luxurious, elegant and expensive your product or service, the more money you should be spending on your literature and brochures. I'm sure that someone thought it a great idea to hire a psychologist, but the psychologist is not a business, branding or salesperson. And this is the challenge that I run into a lot with businesses, they hire these consultancy firms to solve problems that they have no experience or authority in solving. Sales problem = Sales Trainer. Marketing Problem = Marketing Consultant. Simple.

Things that work in theory often do not always translate into the real world of selling. You have to try things for yourself, and if you suspect that things aren't working, don't bury your head in the sand. Apply logic, reason and common sense and 90% of the time you will see for yourself what you need to do in order to solve your own challenges.

You can apply this principle to all areas of your life. Too many people make the mistake of asking for advice from others, when the opinions from others is usually worse than taking your own advice. I personally never ask for advice from anyone, unless I know them to be a World class expert in that relevant field. The same applies to your personal life: never take career or financial advice from someone who earns less than you.

PAPERWORK

Prior to entering your appointment, all of your paperwork should have been pre-prepared and ordered neatly. By paperwork, I mean all the forms and literature you need in order to take your customer through this sales system.

I cannot tell you exactly what paperwork you'll require for your appointments because each industry is different. But I can give you a brief outline of what I would recommend you use and you can adapt this list to your own industry:

- Survey Document (we will cover this shortly)
- Blank paper for writing notes
- Finance paperwork (if your company offers finance/credit)
- List of what the customer will receive
- Testimonials
- Market Comparison (again, we will cover this shortly)
- Offer agreement
- The contract
- Customer satisfaction questionnaire

I always had my salespeople create a pack with all of these documents neatly arranged inside in the order that they come out on the sales presentation. I would also advise that you keep them in your car in a box as well as a dozen or so already made up in your bag. This stops the problem of running out of the correct form at any stage.

As well as these documents above, you also need your glossy brochures, customer welcome packs (for when they become a new customer) as well as many more documents. Just ask yourself the question: If I were a new customer would I be impressed with this literature and brochure(s)?

If the answer to this question is no, then I would suggest you speak with your manager to recommend that the literature be improved. Good literature must be produced by both a graphic designer and a good copywriter. Many businesses make the mistake of thinking they can do this themselves and the results are disastrous. Again, leave the copywriting to a copywriter.

You will also need the following for your appointments:

- Customer testimonials
- A brochure explaining the benefits of your product or service
- Evidence that your product or service does what you say it does
- Any awards that your company, product or service have received
- Any positive media coverage on your product or service
- Legal information on your company that some customers will want to see

I would recommend that you keep all of this in a nice expensive folder in your bag and show your customer right at the beginning. The way I would suggest you do this is to showcase these 'bragging documents' in an informal way. Show that you are the best, but you don't brag about it… this shows true strength and confidence in your product or service.

BAG/BRIEFCASE

The bag you bring to your sales appointments is just as important as the suit you wear. I've lost count of the times that I've seen a well-dressed and attractive man or lady show up for an appointment with a scruffy, falling apart or strange looking sales bag.

I was hired by an extremely successful salesman to coach his wife, who had been selling high-end kitchens (somewhat unsuccessfully). When I met her, what really surprised me about her was that she carried two enormous 40Lb scruffy suitcases around with her into each appointment.

I just couldn't get my head around this at all, yes I understand when selling kitchens that you need to show samples.

But, there is no requirement to show the customer 20 different types of marble worktop. If anything, she was giving the customer too much choice and creating confusion over clarity, but more on this later...

What I want to focus on at this point is the bags she was using, or should I say 'the old suitcases' she was using, which had been given to her by her sales manager. Firstly, I don't think it's appropriate that this lady was asked to carry two 40 lb suitcases on her own, and not because she was a lady, I don't think it's logical for a man to do this either. Your sales bag should only contain your paperwork and forms, and not any bulky or heavy samples.

A good sales professional does not need heavy samples because he or she knows their product or service inside and out. In most cases a glossy brochure showing images of your product or service is more than adequate to make a sale. To this day, I still have people disagreeing with me on this point, and yet each time I demonstrate and test this with their sales team across any industry, their company sales have never dropped and have often INCREASED.

It's all in the system. Now the only caveat to this, is when selling items that NEED to be felt, or touched, such as a luxury fabric for example. If you really must take a heavy sample, then only take 1-3, not a selection.

Your bag need be no larger than 16 inches (40 cm) in length, 12 inches (30 cm) high, and 5 inches (12.5cm) deep, weighing no more than 11 Lbs (5kg). I would recommend a black polished leather effect with chrome clasps to give an elegant image if selling high end products.

By high end, this does not necessarily mean high price, it simply means high quality.

APPEARANCE

To really go into depth on your appearance I recommend you read two more books, one on personal grooming, and the other on your style and dress.

Grooming: it's important that you be as well-groomed as is physically possible. This means paying attention to good hygiene (no body odor), skincare, hairstyle, oral hygiene (teeth, gums, breath), facial hair (men), makeup (ladies), etc. There is nothing worse than someone giving you a presentation face to face, with terrible smelling breath, food in their teeth, cigarette smells, etc. The better your grooming, the more you will sell, it really is as simple as that.

Human beings are visual creatures, we make snap decisions on people based on the way they look, the way they walk, the clothes they wear, the car they drive, the house they live in, and much more.

<u>It's neither right or wrong</u>, it's just the way it is. As one of my mentors used to say: 'It doesn't matter why things are the way they are, they just are, don't waste any energy on it`.

Clothing: the general rule is that it should be simple, attractive, well-fitting and clean. You don't need to purchase expensive designer suits in order to look good and compete with the best. The most important thing is that your suit fits correctly and the colours compliment you effectively.

If you are not required to wear a suit, then your clothing should be appropriate for your industry. To give an example,

I was recently consulting for an engineering company who used to see their clients in suits and then take them through the workshop where all the workers would be pretending to show a classy and clean image wearing nice clothing.

I explained to them that there really was no need to dress in this way, their clients expect them to be wearing the type of clothing that engineers would wear. After some back and forth, they finally took my suggestion on board and their sales went up. Why? The customers said it felt more real to see the workers actually working away, covered in grease and sweating. It felt genuine and gritty.

When I first started out in sales, I didn't have the tailor made suits and shirts, or the handmade leather shoes I have in my wardrobe now.

Having little money, I would walk into a department store and purchase a low cost suit off the rack that was near to my size. I would then take this suit to the local tailor/seamstress and have them take up the trousers and sleeve length. Then they would bring in the back of the jacket slightly and taper the trousers to give a better fit.

This gave the image to my office and customers of me having a tailor made suit. What they didn't know was that it cost a fraction of the price of a real tailor made suit, and you can do the same.

Being successful in sales is not a sprint race, it's more like a marathon...slowly but surely working on yourself and improving your abilities every single day. If you can look back at the end of the week and say you improved something about yourself even if by just 1%, you had a successful week and can be proud of yourself.

Men: I recommend you only wear a navy blue or grey suit for your appointments, and only white, or light blue shirts with French cuffs and simple cufflinks. These colours have been proven time and time again over decades of research and testing to be the most effective for sales appointments, as they are simple, clean and evoke an air of trust about you.

Bright colours can subconsciously signify danger or other unpleasant psychological reactions to your customer.

Ladies: I recommend pastel colours, and to avoid bold yellow, green or pink unless you are selling cosmetics, beauty products, travel services or of a similar industry. A solid and simple coloured suit will always be your best colour choice with a white shirt.

OFFICE

If you host your customers or clients at your office, there are a few golden rules to follow…

Your office needs to be:

- **Extremely clean:** a dirty or dusty office gives off a very bad impression. If I'm ever in a dirty office that hasn't been cleaned recently, it instantly lowers my opinion of that person and company. If they haven't got the time or finance to hire a cleaner to dust their desk, it tells me that the quality of their product/service may be poor too. 'How you do anything is how you do everything`.
- **Minimalistic:** your office must be tidy and free from clutter in order to relax your customer. Whenever I'm in an office and the space or the desk is too cluttered, I find

it very distracting, so I know my customer is distracted too. Cluttered desk = cluttered mind. In this situation, it's best to hold your meeting with your customer away from this environment. I would personally never purchase a service from someone who had a cluttered desk.

- **Well Organised:** A well-organised office shows professionalism and pride in your work. It also builds up more trust with your customer because you will be able to pull up their file instantly as opposed to fumbling around for five minutes, which shows disorganisation and that you haven't prepared or don't really care.
- **Comfortable:** You must have air conditioning in hot weather or heating in cold weather. There is nothing worse than being either too hot or too cold, this is one of the biggest distractions for a customer. You also need to have a comfortable waiting area, with comfortable seating. I would also advise that you have refreshments available including: **coffee, tea, water, soft drinks, fruit, and snacks.** Most businesses provide some type of drinks, but the majority don't provide snacks. If you are a sales professional, like me, you'll have experienced the odd missed meal here and there and I can't think of anything worse than presenting or being presented to, on an empty stomach. Have snacks available for your customers at all times.
  My favorite appointment ever was when I had not eaten since breakfast due to my appointments backing up. My final evening appointment had all sorts of snack items available which I very gladly enjoyed.
- **Style Appropriate:** a customer would expect a solicitor's office to have heavy expensive furniture, where a fashion magazine would be expected to have fashionable and stylish furniture. Make sure the furniture in your office is suited to your profession. If you know you're doing yourself a dis-service hosting clients at

your office, then meet them elsewhere as you only get one chance at a good first impression.
- **Quiet:** there is nothing worse than a noisy office with lots of distractions as this distracts both you and your customer. If you're hosting the meeting at your office, make sure you turn all electronic devices to silent, such as your phone, email, ping notifications, etc. I would also advise that you put a sign on the door that states 'MEETING IN PROGRESS, DO NOT DISTURB' and to also tell other people in the office not to enter the room when you are in a meeting.

Your meeting location is like the cornerstone of your buildings foundation, without integrity, the rest of your presentation just won't stand up.

When meeting business clients, I personally prefer to meet in a small empty boardroom because it's neutral ground and neither of us are going to be distracted or interrupted. There's no clutter on the desk, it's clean, tidy and has exactly what I need in order to give a presentation.

I have seen some weird and wonderful presentations in my day that have involved multiple screens with whiteboards, flip charts, large spiral-bound presentations and much more… It looks quite cool, but was just far too complicated. In most cases, it was my job at the end to simplify it all down, consolidate it using a single piece of paper and a pen showing the facts and figures combined with the benefits, and then close the deal there and then.

The most well-known example of this was when I was called in to finalise a deal that had 'almost' been made, between two technology companies. It took me the best part of three days just to understand the sheer complexity of this deal. When I finally got clear as to what was on offer, I called the board in and presented the way I thought they should present it to the opposing board…

Two days later they did just that and within two hours, the entire deal was wrapped up. Sometimes, it just takes a good sales professional to be able to simply the complex and present it in a very basic way that anyone can understand.

And remember this, if your customer needs to 'think about it' at the end of your presentation, it means that you haven't presented correctly. You can't have done. Because this sales system is designed to cover every basis and angle, there is nothing left to cover or you couldn't have passed one of the steps in the process.

Planning and preparation is key, it's the most important step in this entire process. Without a strong foundation, you can't even start to build your house. I recommend you use this chapter as a guide or checklist and make sure you have these foundations clear in your mind before moving on to the next chapter.

- The more preparation you do, and the more systemisation you add to your daily and weekly routine, the less you have to think about.
- The less you have to think about, the more peace of mind and mental clarity you'll have.
- The better your mental clarity, the more energy you will be able to apply to your sales appointments and the more sales you'll make.
- The more sales you make, the more confident you'll become, the more money you'll earn and the less anxiety

you will feel, which leads to even more confidence!

CONFIDENCE comes from COMPETENCE.

COMPETENCE comes from PRACTISE.

PRACTISE comes from THEORY.

THEORY comes from STUDY.

So study this book hard...

CHAPTER 2

SECTION I: MARKET

SUB SECTION II: BOND

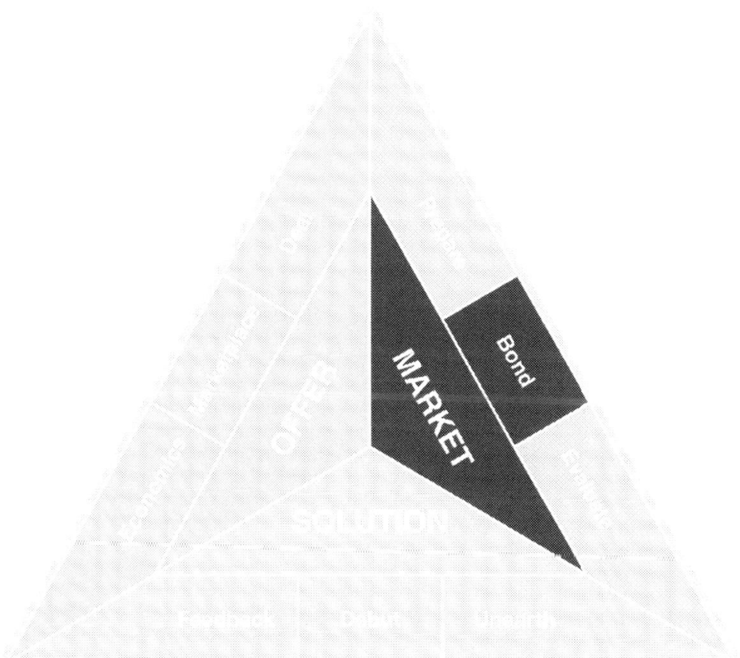

Sales Revolution System™

★★★★★

Many people completely overlook the basics of the bonding/ rapport building stage, downgrading it as having little importance in comparison to the presentation or 'pitch.' But in actual fact, it's the second most important thing you can do in the sales process, and here's why…

The ice break consists predominantly of reptilian brain thinking and analysis, this is all done on a subconscious level by your prospect's brain and they have no control over this process. If you set off any warning or danger signs in your prospects mind, (at the start), it will be like climbing Mount Everest to regain their **TRUST** again.

Selling in this century, is about one simple thing… **RELATIONSHIP BUILDING**. To break this down even further, relationship building is about building: **TRUST**. The more trust you can build into the relationship with your prospect, the more likely it is that you will make a sale.

This point is usually completely overlooked by many sales professionals, it's even overlooked by most sales trainers too. Most of the company sales trainings that I sat in over the years were focused on closing techniques, closing the deal, how to influence the prospect into saying yes, etc.

But this is backwards thinking. If you just build **TRUST** right from the start and show the prospect that you have his or her (or theirs if a company's) best interests at heart, it will be like rolling a snowball down the hill as opposed to up the hill.

This is often very difficult for most sales professionals to get, because it's counterintuitive to the their thought process. Most think that they need to focus all their energy on learning how to close, close, close! So if whilst reading this, it already feels natural to you to focus your energy on building **TRUST** and to sell based on trust, you will be starting miles ahead of your competition.

I use the word competition very lightly, because my mindset is that in sales there really is no competition when you use this system as the companies I work for prove. Think of any company who is crushing it right now, and chances are, they use this sales system and training or something similar.

When you start thinking in terms of competing with others, you take the spotlight OFF the client and put it onto your own EGO. It becomes about YOU instead of about THEM, and once you get into this place, you are no longer following the golden rule of delivering a service that meets your prospect needs. Which means the TRUST has also broken down, which means less sales over the long run.

> **<u>This is your first action point:</u>**
>
> **When greeting your customer, give them a warm, caring, sincere smile from ear to ear, and looking into their eyes, say:**
>
> ***"Hello Sir/Madam/ Mr X / Mrs X / First Name; thank you so much for seeing me, I really appreciate your time."***

This may seem simple, but most salespeople NEVER do this. 9 out of 10 salespeople who I asked why not, replied with things such as: ''I don't want to come across as weird' / 'I think it comes across as creepy' / 'I don't want to seem too keen' / 'I think it shows too much eagerness', etc and the list just goes on and on...

Again this is counterintuitive to your thinking, but it's crucial you do this, so I will build on this now:

Don't break eye contact: if you break eye contact while following this process and asking this question, you will come across as uninterested and incongruent. I have seen it done so many times where a salesperson greets their customer, shakes their hand, says "hi" and then looks away instantly, completely breaking rapport and causing a terrible first impression.

The reason this creates a bad first impression is simple, can you remember a time when you had done something wrong as a child? Then your Mother or Father asked you if you knew anything about it, or worse yet, if YOU DID IT?!

What would we do as children? We would look away; we wouldn't make eye contact and the adult asking the question would know we were lying. The same situation remains true throughout our lives; we distrust people who don't look us in the eye when talking to us. It makes us think they have something to hide and comes across as disingenuous.

You will have heard this saying many times:

'You only get one chance to make a good first impression'

But what you may not know is the science behind this statement. The 'first impression' comes from the reptilian part of your brain (you have three brains, reptilian, mammalian & primate) each of which have their own function.

★★★★★

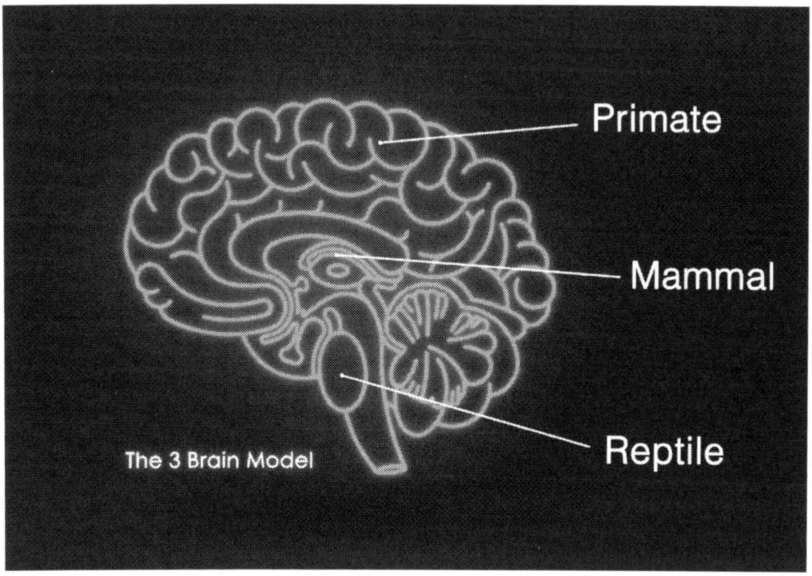

REPTILIAN BRAIN:

Uses **<u>Instinct</u>** for analysis and decision making.

- *Responsibility:* The 4 F's: Flight, Fight, Feed & Fornicate.
- *Role:* Designed to identify dangerous behaviour and incongruent actions in others.
- *Happiest when:* Safe from danger.
- *Evolutionary Role:* Very selfish, and self-centered. Does not have any interest in helping the community to develop and thrive.
- *Location:* Brain Stem
- *Strength:* This brain overrides your mammalian and primate brain.

MAMMALIAN BRAIN:

Uses **Feelings** for analysis and decision-making.

- *Responsibility:* Positive emotions, learning and emotional memory
- *Role:* Assumes the best in people.
- *Happiest when:* Trust, social bonds, higher status present
- *Evolutionary Role:* Community minded, focused on helping the community thrive
- *Location:* Limbic system (Centre of brain)
- *Strength:* This brain is secondary to the reptilian brain.

PRIMATE BRAIN:

Uses **Instinct** for analysis and decision making.

- *Responsibility*: Sensory perception, spatial reasoning, generation of motor commands, conscious thought, intellectual memory.
- *Role*: Vision, predicting
- *Happiest when*: Learning, anticipating future reward, connected to higher purpose.
- *Evolutionary Role*: Predicting brain that helps the community survive
- *Location*: Neocortex (youngest brain)
- *Strength*: Although you would expect this brain to be the strongest, it is actually the weakest!

The Reptilian brain is constantly searching for signs of danger, that's its primary purpose, it doesn't take very much to activate this part of the brain stem either.

I only discovered this information during my first six months of selling when someone had given me a tip about maintaining eye contact and smiling when greeting the prospect. I didn't understand at the time why this was so important, but the more I read up on psychology and human behavior, the more this point made total sense. Prior to this, I would not shake hands, I would not smile, I would just greet my prospect and sit down right away and begin my presentation after a couple of minutes of small talk.

You see, what I had been taught was a sales PROCESS. It was based on logic and designed by a very intelligent person, but intelligence is often the biggest problem that we face in this day and age. We don't need any more intelligence, what we need is more common sense, more people that understand relationship building and trust building in this field; this is what the future needs.

You will notice as you read through this book that I'm both a very analytical person and at the same time I'm very good at building relationships with people and understanding how others think. All this has come through practice and study.

Whenever anybody tells me something, I never believe it right away, I always have to do my own research and test it out for myself and I urge you to do the same as you read through this book. Don't just take what I say word for word, you have to actually practice this for yourself, do your own research and only once you see the point proven, adopt it into your own philosophy.

When it comes to rapport building, you're either going to find this very easy, or very difficult; there aren't many people who fit perfectly in the middle. My ability to build rapport with others was not a natural ability, in fact I used to be terrible at it. I developed this skill through forcing myself to interact with as many people as possible over several years. It was uncomfortable.

One book that helped me to develop this area was called: 'How to Win Friends and Influence People' by Dale Carnegie, which is still to this day one of the bestselling personal development books of all time. I highly recommend you get hold of a copy and read it as many times as you are able, until you feel it has become ingrained into your own philosophy.

To build this mental muscle of rapport building, I advise the following:

Speak to as many people as you possibly can. This doesn't mean prospects. This means when you're waiting in line, talk to the person in front or behind you, you don't even need to say anything of importance, simple small talk will be sufficient. Talk to people wherever you go.

You may be wondering why I'm advising you to do this, what difference does it make?

Well here's the psychology behind it: the difference between those who are effective in rapport building and those who are ineffective comes down to one simple thing: **FEAR**.

I'm not talking about conscious FEAR here like a lion stood in front of you wanting to eat you; I'm talking about your own reptilian brain creating false fear for you as a protective mechanism. This stems from evolutionary psychology from tens of thousands of years ago where if you communicated the wrong thing to the wrong person, the alpha male/chief could attack you and potentially kill you.

It seems silly and completely illogical that this would still exist in the 21st century, but science has proven that time and time again, our brains have not kept up with our environment. Hence why we cram ourselves into cities with millions of other people when there is an abundance of space outside of the Cities. We still operate as pack animals and want to be accepted by the group, we want to be part of the social order; it's ingrained into us.

Human beings are strange creatures, we want to fit in and be part of the social group, but at the same time we want to be different, we want to stand out. We want to be important and be noticed by others which is why we buy designer clothing paying a hundred times the value of the suit, or spending our week's wages on getting our hair done so we look nice.

Even those who are honest about wanting to stand out, constantly find themselves doing the polar opposite so they can fit in with their social group. Can you see the irony in all this?

Please, don't think I'm criticising here, I'm merely pointing out the obvious truth that we either fail to notice or become ignorant of the fact. There is nothing wrong, it's just human nature and the more you understand of this creature called the 'human being', the more you will be able to influence him/her. Even the most senior vice president or CEO is still a human being and cannot escape their brains wiring.

By speaking to as many people as you possibly can, it retrains the reptilian part of your brain, in much the same way as breaking a phobia. The way to break a phobia of public speaking for example is, well, to speak in public, to give presentations, to speak in front of a large audience. You cannot break a phobia by thinking about it; it just doesn't work.

You have to do the thing over and over, as this tells that part of the brain that in doing the action, nothing bad happens. Eventually the brain will eliminate the fear or phobia by realigning your philosophy. Remember that your brain is designed to help you, not hinder you; it holds these false fears as a way to protect you. If you have a phobia of something, it means that somewhere in your deep past an event occurred which was uncomfortable for you as a child. As a result of this, your brain came up with ways to avoid this uncomfortable situation occurring again, in the form of a fear or phobia.

Most of the time you won't even notice it, it's subconscious. I had no idea that I had a fear of swimming until someone pointed out that every time I was asked to go swimming in the lake or sea, go on a boat, go scuba diving, or any water-based sports, I would flat-out decline. I didn't even know that I was doing this, to me it just seemed natural to not want to go near the water.

It was only by looking back at my past childhood that a vivid memory came to me. The memory was quite traumatic, my father had been taking me swimming since I was four or five years old, I loved swimming every Sunday, I even looked forward to it.

But one day when I was about seven or eight years old, I remember swimming at the community pool, when another boy held my head under water and tried to drown me. I tried to scream out and shout for help, but the more I tried the more water I swallowed. It was only because a passerby saw this and saved me that I didn't drown.

From this point on, I had a fear of swimming and water. I

never went swimming with my father again and have only recently started swimming again, once I had observed the traumatic memory and realised that it was no longer helping, but hindering me. If you can just show your brain that the fear is not real and not needed, your brain will let go of it.

The only way to achieve this is to do the things you fear the most as well as finding that initial memory and observing it not as a child, but as an adult which in most cases will dissolve the fear.

My biggest fear in in my late teens and early twenties was of talking to women. Over 90% of the men reading this, will have experienced the same fear during this time period, again it's ingrained into our philosophy to be fearful of talking with women. No amount of reading books will get you over this challenge, despite what many authors will tell you, believe me, I tried!

The way I finally broke this phobia was, yes you guessed it... I went out and spoke to women, despite breaking a sweat each time!

I then reached a point where I could then speak to any woman or man anywhere in the world without an ounce of fear in my body. Combined with going to every social event I possibly could, and talking to people all throughout the day in public places, I reached a point where I can now literally speak to anyone. Again, it all stems from experience...

Coming full circle then, if you have a fear of looking someone deep in the eyes, smiling, and greeting them warmly, it's more than likely due to an unconscious fear of people. And you now know how to overcome this fear, simply by talking to as many people as you possibly can.

The fear WILL subside; it just takes time. You will then notice, how all of your sales interactions just become so much more simple and fluid. People will start to open up to you, they will share their fears and frustrations with you where they won't with most other sales people. They will start to TRUST you, because of your openness and ability of being raw, open and real with them.

CONFIDENCE comes from COMPETENCE

COMPETENCE comes from EXPERIENCE

EXPERIENCE comes from DOING

And in order to DO, you must first UNDERSTAND, and the understanding comes from studying books like this, then creating an action list and then taking that action.

99% people just won't take the action, and that's why they never end up getting any further in life, they just won't take the action.

Success comes at a price, it's not easy, and it takes hard work and effort. No one ever became successful without first working hard for it. And sales is the ultimate challenge, if you master it, you will become wealthy beyond your wildest dreams.

HOW TO BUILD RAPPORT WITH YOUR PROSPECT

At this point, you should have made a note on your action

list to improve your confidence around other people and in talking with other people, as this is the only way to naturally build your rapport skills by following the methods I described above.

You will have heard all the clichés about building rapport with people as soon as you walk into their home/office, so I'll cover a few off now so we can get these untruths out of the way...

- **Giving a huge over the top smile:** this does not build rapport, this makes your prospect slightly wary of you, and the question goes off in their mind: what are they overcompensating for?
- **Spotting a talking piece and 'picking it up':** this does not build rapport, this actually creates the opposite effect as you are touching their possessions and dominating their space. People don't like this. You can talk about it, but don't touch it.
- **Seeing a family photo and asking who this is:** this is an excellent strategy later on in the rapport building process, but you must have built trust first. If you ask this question within the first couple of minutes of meeting your prospect, you will activate their defensive mechanism. Would you ever share personal information on your own family with someone that you had only just met?
- **Giving a really strong handshake:** this stems from the desire to dominate others, or in the prospect's mind, of you trying to dominate them. I'm not sure where this advice initially came from, but to give a really strong handshake is actually <u>incorrect</u>. The pressure of your handshake should match the person with whom you are shaking, never harder, never softer – just equal pressure.

★★★★★

- **Insist on a cup of tea, coffee, water, drink before you even sit down:** the first time I heard a sales trainer teach this rapport building strategy, I thought he was making a joke. Unfortunately, having heard it on several sales training sessions, I found this to be a common teaching. I understand the principle behind this and how it will work in certain situations on certain people, but for the most part, and the majority of the population, this will activate the defensive part of their brain.
  It's a dominating tactic used by old school salespeople, designed to place the salesperson above the prospect in importance. For the prospect to use their time and personal resources in providing for you. This completely goes against the system you are learning in this book.

The best advice I can give you for rapport building is to BE YOURSELF.

What? No Golden Nugget here?

Sure, I could tell you all sorts of tricks and tactics in order to influence and manipulate your prospect to agree with you on certain points… But the fact of the matter is, when I used to do all these things, I never got into true rapport or more importantly TRUST with my customer.

It was only when I was sat with a friend in a coffee shop one day, and we were laughing, joking and having a really pleasant conversation, that it dawned on me…

All this time, I had been trying to build rapport unnaturally, but rapport can't be built UN-naturally. It can only be built from the point of listening to the other person, finding common interests, and then sharing common stories based on those mutual interests. This is how rapport is built, by finding mutual interests, this is where the personal connection is made.

Your job now becomes ten times easier. You no longer have to work hard to find talking points, to force conversation pieces, or ask boring questions. If you come from the point of view of wanting to know:

WHO IS THIS PERSON? AND HOW CAN I HELP THEM TO MAKE THEIR LIFE EASIER?

All of a sudden, you will find yourself falling into rapport without even trying. In fact, the new challenge will become: how to stop them talking about themselves too much so you can start your presentation!

The other great news, is when they talk about themselves, they are giving you plenty of information which you can then use to help them with their buying decision throughout the presentation.

Think of yourself like a detective solving a crime, the prospect is your suspect… Who are they? The first thing the detective would do is to find out as much as possible about their suspect through research. Your job is to do the same.

The second thing the detective would do is to ask the suspect a series of targeted questions in order to find out more about the suspect. Very rarely does the detective launch an all-out assault on their suspect, throwing accusatory remarks their way. They first want to build rapport, because the detective knows that the more trust the suspect places with him or her, the more open they will be during questioning.

★★★★★

This equates to you, the salesperson also building rapport and trust before asking your prospect a series of targeted questions to find out the pains and frustrations they are having with their current product or service. Without being in rapport, none of this would be possible.

The sole purpose of rapport building is to get your prospect to open up to you, to see you as a friend and to trust you. Never abuse that trust as a salesperson.

Trust is your greatest ASSET, and a lack of integrity, your greatest ENEMY.

PROMOTION

Many direct sales companies use a trick called a 'promotion'– which is basically a 'made up' offer that doesn't really exist. When I was first taught about using FAKE promotions on customers, it made me really nervous. The reason it made me really nervous was because I don't like lying. My parents taught me as a child to always tell the truth no matter what and there were harsh punishments in store if I were ever caught lying.

The main problem I had with the fake promotions that 99% of direct sales companies use was that there was just no need for them. Why not just create a real promotion I thought to myself? That seemed the logical solution to me and yet I was always told to "just get on with it, the customer is dumb and doesn't have a clue" by my sales manager.

It's amazing actually looking back, how many times I heard that same statement: "the customer is dumb". No wonder those sales trainers and sales managers never amounted to very much with an outlook and philosophy like that.

★★★★★

For those of you that don't know what a fake promotion is, let me explain using an example from the 'windows and doors/double glazing' sales industry:

Right at the start of the sales presentation the old-school salesman would say something along the lines of... "Mr/Mrs X, the reason I'm here today is to offer you a very special promotion and opportunity. We are only looking for 1 house in this area to become a show home. What this means is "(old school salesman goes on to explain what will be required from the customer)".

"But I have to tell you, you will only get one opportunity to accept this offer at the end of the presentation, so all I need from you is a simple yes or no answer at the end, not 'maybe', not 'I'll have a think about it and let you know', a simple yes or no answer is what is required, are you capable of doing that for me?" The customer then replies with "Yes, I think so" etc.

The salesperson is then taught to really drive this home... "ok well I trust you, I trust you that you'll give me a yes or no answer at the end because you seem like an honest person..."

What this old-school salesperson is looking for is a sign of weakness as well as signs of impulse buying, if the prospect says "yes", it's a green light and they know there is a very high chance of a sale. Now don't get me wrong, I'm not saying that you're wrong for using this technique, that's not for me to judge.

How far you go with your sales 'patter' depends on how far you're willing to manipulate people to your gain. Manipulation isn't always a bad thing, as long as you can see that what you are offering is a lot better than what the prospect currently has and it will dramatically improve their life.

But if you can clearly see that what your prospect currently has is completely fine as it is, and by going with your product or service they're going to now receive an inferior product or service, and at more money; then deep down you should know that this is the wrong decision for the sake of a nice commission check.

The reason you should use a promotion in your presentation again comes down to psychology. People love to feel special, to feel like they're getting something that others aren't getting. It comes back to the principle here that we all want to stand out and feel special, whether that be consciously or subconsciously.

When you present a promotion to your prospect in the correct way, this will hit upon all of these points like a sledgehammer hitting a nail into a piece of wood, it's very unlikely that the hammer (your promotion) will miss the spot. What are the points I'm talking about? Evidence markers, that your prospect has been looking for to back up their belief that they are in some way special.

Here is the correct way to create and explain a promotion to your customer, again I will use the home improvements industry as an example as this makes up a large percentage of the direct sales industry. Please also note that this example is based on a B2C (Business to Customer) environment as opposed to a B2B (Business to Business) environment. For those of you reading who are in a B2B environment, you can simply take this example and create your own type of promotion for your desired customer:

"What we're offering for a select amount of homeowners in this area is the opportunity to partner with us on a special promotion we're running. The good news is, I wouldn't be sat here if you didn't already meet that criteria, so that's the hardest part over."

What I've said here is, the keywords 'select amount', straight away this tells the prospect, that they have an opportunity here that is quite rare and limited, which creates intrigue in their mind. It's the same thing that Ferrari do with their cars, they create scarcity and rarity, much like the principle behind the antique industry.

Antiques are valuable and rare, because they are limited in supply; it really is that simple.

The next point, is the keywords: 'opportunity to partner with us', notice here how I'm not going in strong and saying 'you can buy this from us', because when you say you can buy this from us, in their mind, people say "no thanks". But when you say the words 'opportunity' it stirs that part within us that likes excitement and raises the question 'what opportunity?`

And finally, I've told them that they meet a select criteria and that meeting the criteria was extremely difficult. With all these points combined, the prospect is now both excited and anxious to know more.

"The promotion really is simple Mr/Mrs X, in return for a heavy discount on our (product or service), all we ask for from you in return is: (then insert your criteria, make sure you make it easy for them to meet this criteria). An example would be:

1. We would like to take a photograph of the beautiful work we have completed in your home.
2. We would like a testimonial from you, stating how great you found our service, which we can take quickly over the telephone, or you can just tell us in the house after the work is complete, it should only take a couple of minutes.
3. We would like to track how much energy you have saved from your electricity bill with this new energy-saving solution that we are going to install for you. How do you feel about those three things that we would ask from you in return for a large discount?

- Keywords: 'large discount', this speaks for itself, who doesn't like large discounts?
- 'All we ask for from you in return is', we are down-playing this by making it clear that the prospect really doesn't have to do much at all in order to receive this 'large discount'.
- Notice how all three points are simple, and non-obtrusive. Everything is downplayed and the third point is even dressed up as a benefit to show that there is an after sales service
- Finally, I am asking the customer "how do you feel about those 3 things?", notice that I'm not saying "what do you think?". When you ask someone, what do you '**think**', people will often lie to you. But when you ask someone how do you '**feel**', in most cases they will tell you the truth.

And even in the rare case when they don't tell the truth, their body language and facial expressions will give them away because the feeling brain is incapable of deception.

There are two more powerful things to add in to your presentation here just before you move forward, and they are: **Charts & Testimonials.**

Charts are a really powerful tool, which are hugely underutilised in the sales industry. My presentations would always have two or three simple and easy to understand charts. Notice I say 'simple' and 'easy to understand' – this is key! Most salespeople who work in a more technical industry assume that they need to make their sales process more technical, not true.

It's actually quite the opposite. The more simple your presentation, the smarter your prospect feels, to the point where they often think you are below them in terms of status and intellect – this is a good thing. I always want my prospect to think they are smarter than me, as they then feel like they are in control of the presentation. As long as you can manage this effectively, you will have a green light the whole way through...

Humility is one of your greatest assets as a salesperson, the smarter you treat your prospect, the kinder they treat you.

One thing to notice with intelligent people, especially in technical sales such as IT, is that they are often completely overwhelmed with the amount of brainpower they are using each day. And it's a huge breath of fresh air to be able to sit through a very simple and easy presentation where they don't have to try to work everything out themselves.

The more simple and easy it is for them to understand, the more likely they are to buy from you because you make their job so simple. And that's the key here; the easier you make it for someone to buy from you, the more likely it is that they WILL buy from you.

This is why it's so important to use simple graphs. People love graphs, graphs are so simple and easy to read and understand data that it makes their decisions easier to make.

Your graphs should show the main benefits from a measurable point of view. However, be aware that some of the benefits that your product or service provide *are not measurable*. An example of this might be the 'feeling' of success you would feel by driving a luxury car, this would not be something that you would use a graph for, in this case, you would use a test drive so they 'feel' it for themselves.

But if driving that same car Vs an average everyday car would save your customer 50% in monthly fuel costs, this would be something that you would plot on a graph as measurable.

Graphs are hugely important, and you will find out why towards the end of the book.

The second important tool or resource to present here for the first time are **testimonials**. Many sales trainers will tell you that testimonials come at the END of your presentation. This is again, not correct.

Your **testimonials** should be scattered throughout your entire presentation, popping up here and there at key points.

The first time that your testimonials should make an appearance is towards the end of stage 2. At this point you merely pull out the testimonials for 'social proof'; the idea here is to use them in a relaxed way. The idea is not to have your customer read all of your testimonials; that comes later. At this stage, you merely want to show your testimonials for social proof so that your prospect becomes more open to hearing what you have to say.

Imagine if someone came to speak with you about something that you were skeptical about, would you give them your full attention? Probably not. But if they produced a folder full of glowing testimonials, you would now become more receptive to hearing what they had to say.

The idea here is to show the testimonials, but not go into detail, for that comes later. Here's an example of a good testimonial:

> ***"Neil McCoy-Ward is quite simply one of the most impactful sales trainers we have ever hired in the last 5 years. His training added over £5M in sales over a 12 month period, we can't recommend him highly enough and we will certainly invite him back over and over again."***

Your testimonial should be kept simple and to the point, your prospect doesn't want to read an essay. They just want to know what benefit others got from your product or service. Don't over complicate any of this system, it really is very straightforward.

At this point, your prospect will have given you the green light to proceed in your presentation. It is at this point we now move on to the next step in this process, which is to Evaluate.

CHAPTER 3

SECTION I: MARKET

SUB SECTION III: EVALUATE

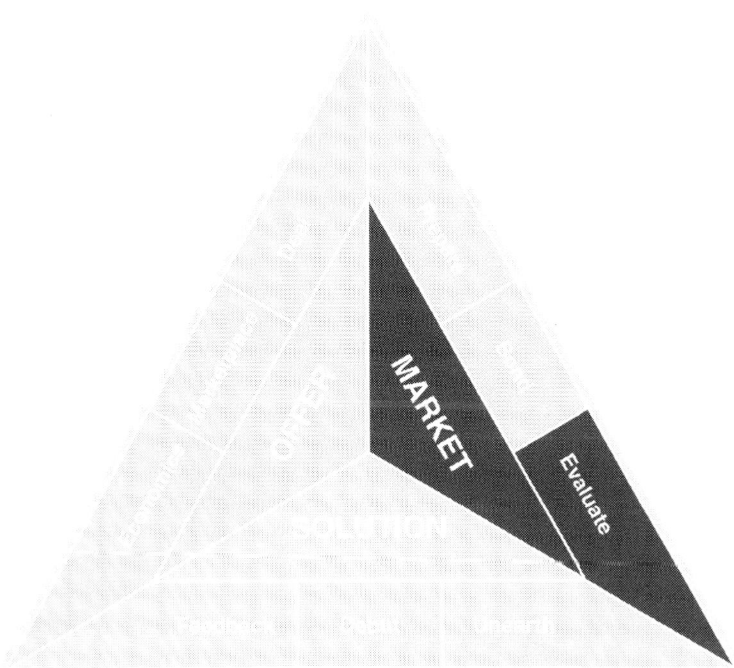

Sales Revolution System™

This stage should be thought of more as the **'information collection'** stage.

It amazes me the amount of times I see a prospect stood in front of a salesperson, that either had a) no interest whatsoever in purchasing their product, or b) was very interested in purchasing their product, so much so in fact that they may as well have been waving their credit card in their face. And yet, in both cases, the salesperson wasted an enormous amount of their time and energy, purely because they did not stop to ask the correct 'qualifying' questions.

If a prospect can see that the salesperson is clearly incompetent and/or too lazy to find out their needs and requirements, the prospect will not place an order with that salesperson even if they were ready to buy. In almost every case, the prospect would walk away and place their order with a more deserving salesperson.

To give you a real-life example of this, I was recently looking to purchase a new car and had three manufacturers in mind. When I walked into the first dealership, I was stopped from walking around and looking at the models in a very stern way by the receptionist, I was then told to sit down in the waiting area and wait for a 'salesman.'

Firstly, there were several sales 'men' and 'women' stood around the coffee machine laughing and joking, none of which approached me as they clearly saw me entering the front door; this was their first mistake. The second mistake; was the grilling I received from the salesman once I finally got to his desk.

What amazed me the most, was how he didn't build any

rapport with me whatsoever, and yet thought it completely reasonable to ask me for all of my personal details and information including home address and phone number. Needless to say I did not make a purchase from this dealership!

The second dealership I entered was much better, I was greeted warmly by the receptionist and she asked the qualifying question: "how can we help you today Sir?" A perfect start. She then went and got me a very refreshing drink (good), whilst I waited for a 'salesperson' (bad), that was the first mistake.

Regardless of the industry you are in, you should never call yourself a 'salesperson', even if you are one! The word 'salesperson' creates a negative connotation in the customer's mind because it already implies the sale, and/ or people just don't like salespeople; they are perceived as slimy and lacking in integrity.

In most cases people are 'just looking' and will only make a purchasing decision when they are ready. And even if someone is coming to you to make a purchase, it makes no difference; they still don't want to deal with a salesperson. For this reason, you should call yourself something different, such as a 'Consultant' or similar. All of my sales people are called customer service representatives and consultants.

The third dealership very almost got my money; they were very close indeed! I don't mind saying that this dealership was Jaguar Cars, a car brand that I have loved since I was a child as my father spent his whole career designing these cars. He would bring home prototype drawings and he even once brought home an actual supercar, the XJ220.

★★★★★

Again, it started very well; I was greeted warmly by the receptionist and offered a seat and refreshments. This dealership felt different to the other two, it felt more comfortable and welcoming which I liked. I was then approached by the salesman who sat with me in the seating area where we sat and had a drink and made small talk.

He came across as very nice and genuine and did a good job of building rapport. Where he went wrong, was again, not allowing me to walk around and look at the cars. He insisted on going through a long and boring process at his desk and after 20 minutes, I was bored stiff and was losing the will to live!

Then he made the biggest mistake, he took me to their top of the range model and had me sit inside whilst telling me boring facts about the car. Firstly, I was not interested in that style of sports car; I don't care about speed and performance, and never have.

My interest was in a luxurious vehicle with five doors, which I had told him several times – he just didn't listen. If he had just listened to what I was looking for in the first place, and spent some time answering my questions, he would have received the sale from me that same day. Especially as I was there to make a purchase as I had already done my research online.

Six months later, I was driving by the same Jaguar car dealership and saw a beautiful car that caught my eye from the side of the road. I drove in, parked up and checked out the car, it was everything I was looking for and because it was 'used approved', it was half the price of a new car even though it was 3 years old and only had 13,000 miles on the clock, unbelievable.

★★★★★

I looked for a salesperson and a very friendly gentleman came to greet me who looked after the 'used approved' cars. From start to finish, I felt as though I were talking with a friend who had my best interest at heart. He asked me all the correct qualifying questions right the way through the process and gave me the opportunity to actually ask questions too.

It wasn't a boring interrogation; it was warm, friendly and great fun. Sure, at the end he went in for the kill on closing the deal, but I would have expected nothing less from him, he had earned the right to do that! Needless to say, I paid cash for that car the very same day and returned the next day to pick up and drive that car home with me.

This is the power of correct qualifying QUESTIONS combined with the SURVEY.

The transition from Stage 2 to Stage 3 (Bond to Evaluate), is designed to be smooth and unobvious. I have designed it in a way to make it a continuation of the Rapport Building and Promotion stage. Most sales people spend far too much time in Bonding, trying to build rapport. I have heard it said by many a sales trainer that you should spend at least one hour in rapport building.

I completely disagree with this statement on so many levels and have now reached a point where I no longer waste my energy debating this ridiculous philosophy.

★★★★★

The way you build LONG STANDING rapport is not by chatting and making small talk with your prospect. The way you build rapport is by being professional, showing that you have their best interests at heart and helping them to solve their problems or make their life easier.

This is why I push forward from Bond, to Evaluate in a quick and efficient motion, my time is valuable as is my prospects, we are both there for a set reason, and that reason is not to socialize.

I emphasize this point here so strongly because I see and hear the contrary every day, which I find baffling. Decades ago, this method of staying in the rapport stage by making small talk for over an hour would have worked just fine, because it was a different culture back then.

But now, times have changed and people are very busy. They just don't have the time to sit around and make small talk, they have so many decisions to make every day that people have had to become more efficient with their time.

There is no point in getting frustrated about this as a salesperson, all you can do is to adapt your presentation to suit the needs of your prospects and that is what you should be doing every day anyway.

There are usually five very important qualifying questions that you MUST know the answer to before starting your presentation, please add them to your own presentation.

These consist of the following:

Question 1: Is the person sat in front of you the primary decision maker?

The reason you need to know this, is because many a time in my early days, I would go through a full presentation only to be told at the end that they would need to speak to 'person X' for a decision, which really frustrated me. On probing further I discovered that the person I had been presenting to this entire time did not have the authority to make the purchasing decision.

This happens a lot in a B2B environment as well as with older members of the general public. Many people who you deem to be prospects are actually just time wasters, the time waster is your biggest enemy for they will sit through an entire presentation just for the fun of it to improve their own knowledge on a subject with no regard for the sales professionals valuable time.

After this happens to you several times, like me, you will no doubt build a set of questions that identifies the time waster at the outset, thereby allowing you to walk away gracefully and use your time more wisely on someone who is looking for your product or service. You are not only looking out for the time waster, you are also looking to identify whether or not the person sat in front of you is able to make a buying decision on their own.

A perfect example of this is the husband and wife team in every marriage. They will swear blindly that either one of them can make the buying decision on their own (on say a type of home improvement like a new bathroom or kitchen), and to just proceed with the presentation without one of them present.

However, this is not true and you should never present in this situation. If the product or service you are presenting will affect both the husband and wife, they must both be in attendance to hear your presentation.

If either one of them is not in attendance, you must reschedule the appointment for another day when both will be present; failing to observe this point will result in hours of wasted time for you. If you do proceed with your presentation, I guarantee you that 8 times out of 10, the party present, will say these magical words: "Sorry I can't make a decision today, I need to check with my wife/husband/partner, etc."

Once this occurs, and the person who sat through your presentation takes this information to their partner, the partner is now dealing with secondhand information. Because they were not present to hear the entire presentation, they will only receive the key snippets. And from these key snippets, they will only be interested in one thing:

HOW MUCH DOES IT COST?

Without hearing your presentation, (which justifies the cost), the missing party will make the wrong decision based on the watered down information they have just received.

The same plays true in a B2B scenario, over 80% of the sales people I have worked with told me how they had been given information that led them to believe the person they were presenting to was the decision-maker in the company.

However, it only became apparent at the end of the meeting, that the person they had presented to did not have the purchasing authority and was told by a superior to "hear what this salesperson has to say, and report back to me on the facts and figures." This is no different to the household couple.

The person you have presented to is now going to pass on 'secondhand information` to their superior. There will be no emotion attached to these facts and figures as there was with your sales presentation.

In which case, there was no point in delivering a presentation, you may as well have just sent a one-page document outlining the numbers from the get-go and saved yourself the travel and presentation time which was probably considerable.

This is why I recommend having an excellent brochure, because a brochure will save you a LOT of your precious time as you can have your office send these out for you. If someone calls back from your brochure, great, if not, you've lost nothing. And if someone does call you in for a meeting, they are much more likely to have the purchasing power to make a decision.

Your TIME is your most valuable asset, you must use it wisely and guard it against those who would try to steal it from you.

In a B2B sales role, you must thoroughly research the person who you are presenting to beforehand and you must pre-qualify this person to ensure that they are the decision-maker. At the very minimum the person you're presenting to should be no more than one step down from a decision maker.

★★★★★

There have been a number of occasions where I have sat in on multi-million Pound/Euro/Dollar business deals where there were not only two stages but three to five stages in order to get a final decision; this can be common in the big leagues of million dollar deals upwards.

Question 2: Do you have any plans to move locations?

(This question is only relevant if you are selling a big-ticket product that must be installed such as a new network server, or an expensive air-conditioning system as an example.)

I was hired to coach a failing B2B sales team recently and from the feedback I received, they had started to see drastic improvements in their sales. Because of this, I was asked to come back to help consult and close a large contract that they were struggling to close.

I'll never forget the events that unfolded that cold winter evening, because it will stick in my mind forever as an unfortunate failure by their sales manager.

The team had gone through Stage 1, the 'Prepare' (planning and preparation) process in detail over several weeks until they felt they had built up a good enough picture of the target company. They had presented to the first decision maker and were now in the final position to present to the CEO, COO & CTO of the company for the ultimate decision.

Up until this point, five people had worked on this project for the best part of two weeks in total. The contract was worth close to 700,000 Euros with a recurring service contract of 120,000 Euros per year.

I had now been asked to come to sit in on the presentation, advise and to help close the deal should the team be unsuccessful (being as this team were consultants and not professional sales people). The presentation ran smoothly throughout, but I started to notice very unusual body language and facial expressions from the board (showing something was wrong.)

This puzzled me, and I could see the team had missed these signs, and instead of pausing to allow the director to speak, they just ploughed ahead looking for the close. It was at this point that I started to read over their planning and preparation notes and I noticed a couple of discrepancies... As I was there as a consultant, it was not my place to interrupt their presentation, so I allowed them to continue.

Eventually, the CTO held up his hand and asked them to stop. He explained that this product was not suitable for them as they were about to relocate that area of the business to another country!

You could have heard a pin drop in that room.

Had the sales team simply asked the qualifying question at the start, "do you have any plans to move locations (or in this case) to outsource this part of your business either now or in the near future?" This entire situation could have been avoided.

Unfortunately there was no way to recover from this heavy blow, as to compete with their new figures would have meant less than a 5% profit margin which was just unworkable. I felt terrible for my client as it was a huge financial blow to them in two weeks of lost work and losing the contract.

★★★★★

Question 3: What Product or Service are you currently using?

The answer to this question will tell you what you are up against in terms of competition. If you are a true 'professional' salesperson, you should know each of your competitors and the product/service they offer. A failure to know this information will result in you blindly pitching the benefits of your product or service, which could be inferior to that which they are currently in possession of.

Obviously, this will result in a failure to make the sale, as well as your wasted time and embarrassment. You must know the WEAKNESSES as well as the strengths of your product or service, because in many cases, your customers will.

If you know that you have weaknesses in your product, you can use this point to your advantage during the presentation by explaining how this is being improved currently and will soon be better than the competition. You should address this if, and only if, it is first raised by the customer.

Question 4: Have you looked into this area or done any research yet?

The reason you ask this question is because let's face it, 95% of salespeople beef up their product or service to make it seem like the Ferrari of the car world, even if it's more like a 20 year old banger that needs a kick to start…

I was once sat on a presentation where the salesperson was quite obviously beefing up the product by stating it would do things, that quite clearly it just couldn't. Yet the prospect he was pitching to really did not understand the intricacies of this product and so simply just believed everything the salesperson said to them (which again, is common).

At the end of the presentation as the contract was being signed, I had a feeling in my gut that once the delivery was made, the order would be canceled because it just couldn't do what he said it would do. Close to three months later, this exact thing happened. Not only did his company lose a significant order, but they also now had stock in their storeroom that they have to shift as it was holding up other orders.

To really cap it off, I was called upon by the sales director in my office where he asked me with that salesperson, "did he or did he not say the product could do XYZ…" I didn't want to cause a problem for the salesperson but as my integrity was in question, I had to tell the truth, and as a result of that meeting, unfortunately that salesperson lost his high paying job within the company.

By finding out exactly what your prospect knows about your industry/product/service, you can avoid several problems that come with beefing up your product/service and what it can do. Because in my opinion, exaggerating on what your product or service can do will always come back to bite you.

Just as in the example above, your prospect WILL complain if the product/service does not do what you said it would do. And secondly, I have also seen it on many occasions where the salesperson exaggerated what the product/service could do and unfortunately because they had not asked this qualifying question, the prospect had called them out as being a liar as their knowledge was superior to the salesperson.

By knowing the exact level your prospect is at in terms of

their knowledge, you have prepared yourself for the interaction to come. A good analogy of this is the overly-confident military general (the un-professional salesperson), he believes foolishly that he can defeat anyone, and thus does no research on his opponent. When it comes time to fight, he is defeated by a more prepared yet inferior foe.

We now come to the professional general, (the professional salesperson). He knows that he must be at the top of his game, and his knowledge of his opponent (market competition) & (what does the prospect know?) must be exceptional. Because he had prepared himself thoroughly, he is able to win the battle with ease.

There are too many overly confident 'generals' in our profession who foolishly believe that they can just turn up and win without preparation; this is obviously absurd and the road to failure.

Without asking this question you are just fumbling around in the darkness without a light.

Question 5: What does your current Product/ Service Cost you?

Once you know who your competition is, what they charge and what your prospect already knows about your product and service, things become a lot easier for you. In fact, they become simple…

If your prospect knows nothing about your industry, except that they are paying 'X' and you are offering your product for less, plus you are giving them more benefits, this is the information they now have in order to make a decision. If you've also ascertained that they are the primary decision maker and you've raised their emotional level high enough, it's very likely that you will receive the sale from the customer.

If however, you don't ask this question and only find out at the end that you are offering your product for 'X' and your competition is offering the exact same product for '1/2 X', and your prospect is happy with their current supplier, then you have just wasted your time. This is why asking the right questions is so important before you even start your presentation.

These five questions above form what I believe to be the most important questions that you must receive a positive answer to before even considering going through a presentation with someone. These questions will save you not only a lot of time, but also a lot of frustration, which is on the negative spectrum of emotions. And when you are on the negative spectrum of emotions, it's very difficult to stay positive and make a sale. **Selling is a game of emotions**.

Although I have listed these five questions above, they are just the foundation questions. For each industry you will have many more questions which are outside the scope of this book. My recommendation would be to create your own list of questions based on the top reasons that the prospect turned down your proposal (excluding cost which we will cover later.)

Action Point: Create your own list of qualifying questions.

CHAPTER 4

SECTION II: SOLUTION

SUB SECTION I: UNEARTH

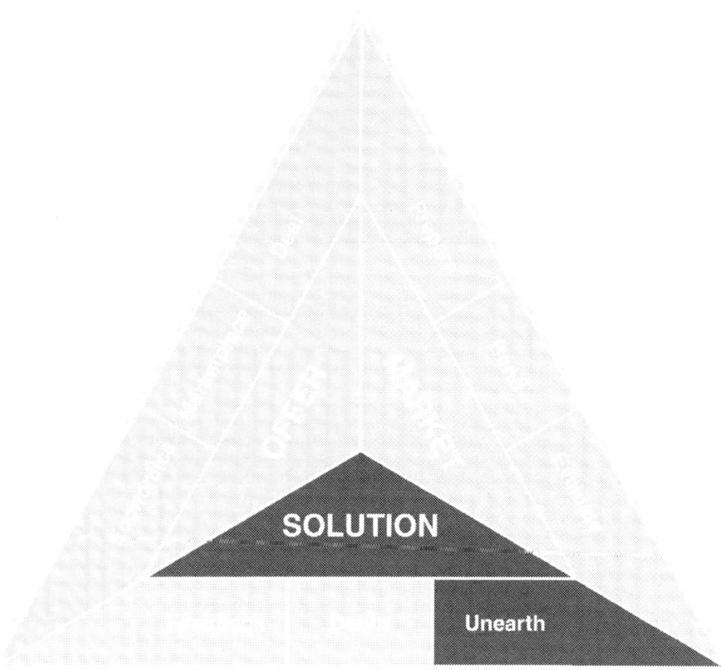

Sales Revolution System™

★★★★★

The next part of your sales process is to conduct an accurate analysis of where your prospect is currently, for only once you know the starting point, can you reach the end goal with precision. In this section, I want you to think of yourself as a detective, your job is to collect as much information as possible so that you can accurately make a solid case based on facts and evidence.

For this example I will use the IT security industry:

At this point, I have already asked my **five** qualifying questions and received positive answers, which have enabled me to now start my presentation…

The first question I would ask is as follows…

"Sir/Madam, how do you feel about spending X thousand per month on your IT security?"

- Because I have asked 'how do you **feel**' I will now get an honest response.

They will respond with something along the lines of:

"Well, it's a lot of money, but we need to protect the security of our clients data from breaches."

- I would now respond with: *"I completely understand, in fact the majority of companies I sit with say exactly the same thing. I'm just looking at these figures here, and I'm amazed at how much more you're paying than the other companies I have seen this week, it's astonishing really."*
- At this point I have now put doubt in their mind, they will begin to question the amount they are spending and

wonder if they are indeed paying too much, because if so, they could get in trouble with their boss for not doing the correct due diligence. I would then proceeded to say: *"but don't worry, it's my job to make sure that you have the absolute best protection, whilst at the same time, getting a superior service for less money, how does that sound to you?"*

They will always reply with a positive answer here, because who wouldn't want these benefits?

I have placed the seed of doubt in their mind, whilst at the same time explaining that I have a superior service. I have also now received permission from them to proceed. I can now probe deeper with my questioning because I have shown that I'm looking out for their best interests; he/she will now feel a strong rapport and trust with me.

From here I start to ask questions regarding the challenges they are currently having with their service. At this point I'm in **data collection** mode, I'm furiously writing down everything they are telling me so that I can use it later, much like a good detective. Of course, it's important not to forget to ask what things they like about their current supplier so I can use this too by showing that my service also has this benefit.

Once you have collected all of this data, it's time to probe deeper with your own set of questions, which again, only you can make based on your industry (so make a note on your action list to create these questions.)

The reason you need all of this data, is because without it, you will just present your product or service in a generic way, much like the car salesman did to me. But, had he only asked what it was I wanted in a car, and then set about delivering a presentation TAILORED to me with all of my requirements met, there would be no reason for me not to purchase the car. The same principle reigns true across every industry, every service and every product.

Find out what the prospect wants, then go about showing them how they can get it, but more importantly, how they can afford it.

The third thing the detective would do after stages one and two, would be to collect the evidence and put it all together. No computer can do this for them, and the same is true for you in your role as a salesperson. The problem-solving ability of a salesperson comes from EXPERIENCE. You must gain this experience the hard way by DOING.

Another good way to create your list of questions, is to think about all the problems that are common in your industry, here are a few examples:

- PRICE/COST
- Poor quality
- Slow manufacturing time
- High maintenance
- Servicing costs
- Legal restrictions
- High manufacturing costs
- Fuel costs
- Inefficiency
- High delivery price
- Slow delivery time
- Poor customer service
- The high price of the product itself

* Poor communication skills
* Antiquated ways of doing business
* Slow to make changes
* Slow response time
* Dominated by big players
* Restrictions on what can be done
* Incompetence
* Poor communication systems

What are the main problems for customers in your industry?

Write these down now; we'll use your answers in the next section...

Great, now you have your frequent problems list, you can start to create a list of questions that you can ask your prospect. Here's an example:

Salesperson: "Mrs X, is there anything that you don't like about your current IT Security supplier?"

Mrs X: "Well, they do a good job most of the time, but I don't expect everyone to be perfect, some of the things they do annoy me a little bit..."

Salesperson: "Oh really? Such as?"

Mrs X: "Well, we're all really busy around here and sometimes we have to chase up security reports from them, which is frustrating as we keep asking them to send the report every Monday, but a lot of times, they don't."

Salesperson: "Oh really, that does sound difficult, because I'm sure that like me, you need that information quickly in order to move your own tasks forward..."

I could continue all day with this, I think you get the idea at this point... Usually once a prospect starts to list off all the things they don't like about their current supplier, they can't stop talking, so just let them carry on. Your job is to keep taking notes and asking more questions until you feel you have enough leverage to 'make your case' at the end of the presentation.

Sometimes it can be difficult to get your prospect to tell you the things they don't like about the current supplier, either because they've been taught not to talk badly of others, or because they're worried it may get back to their supplier that they've talked badly about them.

The technique you can use here, is to say *"whatever you tell me will be kept in the strictest of confidence and will not go anywhere else outside of this room."* This is usually enough to get even the toughest of people to open up a little. Either way, just keep building rapport and asking softer questions, they will eventually start to answer your questions.

Never try to force someone to answer questions if you can clearly see that they are uncomfortable doing so, in this situation, you will do more harm than good and will not only break rapport, but you will also lose their trust. Just continue with your presentation, and gradually ask soft questions about their current supplier as you go through the steps. This is not gossip, it's important fact finding.

The longer you spend with your prospect, the more rapport and trust is built, just don't try to force the prospect or make them feel uncomfortable in any way.

Additionally, notice how I'm not saying after everything she tells me she doesn't like, ***"Oh that's terrible! Well we don't do that!" "We can deliver a better service than they can!"***

Whenever I hear a salesperson doing this, it makes me cringe. This is known as 'butt kissing`, and no one likes a 'butt kisser.` The 'butt kisser` comes across as slimy and incongruent and will smile at your face, and then talk badly behind your back as soon as you've turned around. They can't be trusted and everyone knows this... I'm sure you've met someone like this before.

When your prospect is going through their gripes, your job is to simply sit there quietly, nodding in parts. The occasional, ***"mmm, mmm, yeah"*** in agreement with what they are saying is also appreciated at certain points.

Remember, your job for this entire stage is simply: DATA COLLECTION.

CHAPTER 5

SECTION II: SOLUTION

SUB SECTION II: DEBUT

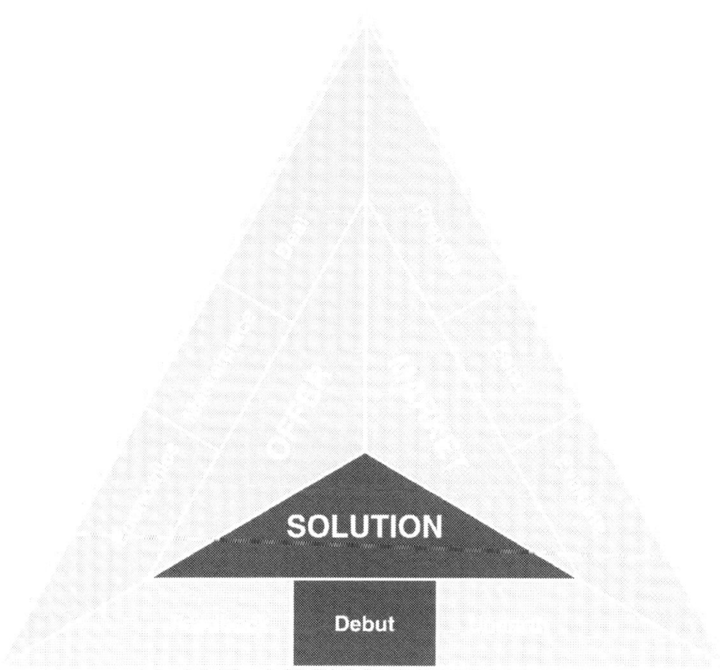

Sales Revolution System™

★★★★★

Stage 5 is all about your company, or more importantly, showing the benefits and credibility of your company. Where most salespeople go wrong in this area is by using their company credibility to sell their product, but prospects don't buy products based on the company credibility.

Prospects only buy products based on how effectively the product solves their problem.

Don't fall into this lazy trap which I see a lot of salespeople doing, because it's very difficult to get out of once you're in it.

Yes, having a strong company brand behind you will make your life easier, it will even help you to sell more product as many people will already trust the brand. Take Apple for example; do you think the Apple salespeople find it difficult to explain how big the brand is? Of course not; but not everyone has this luxury.

Most salespeople have been hired for the exact opposite reason, because the brand isn't well known. If it were, chances are, the company may not need sales people (or at least not as many salespeople), instead the company would have more marketing and customer service people to handle enquiries coming in like Apple do. Have you ever received a cold call from Apple? No, me neither.

The most important part of the company presentation is simply to find out what your prospect 'already knows' about your company. If they don't know anything, then this is where you can really shine. If they have heard good things, even better. But if they have heard bad things, no problem.

★★★★★

Because you can find out exactly what it is they've heard and then use effective questioning and objection handling to overcome these apparent 'bad reviews'.

There are very few challenges in sales that cannot be overcome through a carefully structured presentation.

Remember to build a presentation folder on your company that you can show your prospect (as discussed in Stage 1). Whatever you do here, don't ask your sales manager to make you a presentation folder or worse yet, to give you the 'company approved' edition! In 99% of cases, this will be terrible and will actually lose you sales!

The company edition will usually be full of boring facts and figures, such as the date the company was formed, who the directors are, what industry sectors they operate in, with pictures of important people smiling or pointing at random things such as buildings, etc… All of this is completely irrelevant to the sales presentation, regardless of what anyone in management above you says.

When I was still in my first few months, my sales manager handed out the new company literature on the Monday morning meeting, I took one look at it and stood up to voice my objection immediately. Like any bad sales manager, I was told to "shut up and sit down", because I was 'creating a bad vibe throughout the sales teams!' This seemed to be the thing that was said to me every time I stood up to speak actually...

There is a big difference between complaining for the sake of complaining and complaining because you are concerned about your income. It's important to always stand up and speak your mind in these situations, a good boss will respect that, a bad boss will berate you. Although, there is often a time and place to make complaints, which is usually in private to save the manager any embarrassment.

If you are in a management role, the more you listen to your people on the ground, the better they will sell. Salespeople just want to be listened to and to get some attention and praise from time to time.

I recently attended a 'motivational' speech by the director of a Fortune 500 company. Now firstly, I know this director personally, and he's no motivational speaker as I keep telling him as his mentor! Unless you're a trained professional speaker, it's best to leave this type of speech to the experts.

He had plenty of passion, but this wasn't transferred to the audience (his thousands of employees), purely because he gave a boring history lesson on the timelines of the company. The aim of his speech I later found out, was so that his employees and salespeople could relay these facts and figures during interactions with customers.

It just goes to show that even the people at the top get it wrong from time to time, but that's business. We all make mistakes, but what makes the difference is making a mistake and learning from it. To use it as a lesson and learn from it for the future.

Picture the scene; you are the senior buyer within an engineering or manufacturing company. You have incredibly tight deadlines to hit, and you're massively understaffed (sound familiar?)

★★★★★

You receive a phone call from a very friendly salesperson who would like to come in to speak with you about their line of machinery, and how they can save you money. (I added in the last part about saving money, because most phone calls includes the first but leave out the latter, which is why they don't get the appointment), so for ease, I added in a benefit at the end…

At the meeting you are very excited to hear what this lovely salesperson has to say. You let them know that you only have 30 minutes as time is very tight today due to strict deadlines and being short staffed. The salesperson, then begins by telling you the history of their company, when it was first established, how Mr. X came up with this genius idea followed by a timeline to the present date of what has happened within the company.

Forget everything you know about sales for a moment, and look at this with a logical perspective. What exactly is it that you, the buyer wants' from the salesperson?

You want to know whether or not this salesperson has a product or service that can **a).** Make your life easier, **b).** Save your company money, and **c).** Make you look good to your boss, especially if you are able to source a superior machine at a lower price.

Other than these two points, you, the senior buyer is not interested in anything else the salesperson has to say. You, the senior buyer, are certainly not interested in receiving a history lesson on this salesperson's company! Who cares?!

Does that make sense? I know it seems obvious, but I really need to drill this point in, as this is the stage that I receive the most resistance on when talking to salespeople and sales managers. For some reason, logic goes out the window and they are convinced that they need to give the prospect a history lesson on their fantastic company. But as you've just discovered, the prospect couldn't care less about the company.

So, what exactly should this presentation folder on the company look like? Or a better question yet: what should it contain?

Below, I have listed a general format of pages. Depending on your industry, you may need to include some more technical certificates or specifications, which are outside the scope of this book.

Page 1: A single page document with no more than a few paragraphs on the company. Include the company logo here as well as the company address, and any legal bits of information such as the company registration number, date of formation, etc. Remember, we don't want an essay here...

Like so:

- Company Logo & Mission Statement
- Company Established in 1990
- Registered Address: 123 Knights Tower, London, England, SW1 2BA
- Company Registration Number: 12345678
- Etc...

It's important here to ask the question:

> ***"What do you already know about our company Mr/Mrs X?"***

If they have heard nothing about your company: it's important to spend a little bit of time here talking about your company and building credibility. This is really important because people don't often buy products and services from a company that they know nothing about.

The majority of people will either want to see evidence of copious amounts of other people who have bought your products or services (testimonials), tons of data (graphs), or receive a referral from someone they trust. This is exactly why you will use the pages as shown above, because you are hitting on all of these points: data (graphs = proof), testimonials (other people similar to them like it) & media / PR (if the media are covering it, then it must be good!)

If they have heard <u>GOOD</u> things about your company: you don't need to spend a long time talking your company up here. I would advise you still go through the pages of the presenter above, but you don't need to go into detail, you can just skim over a lot of it in a couple of minutes...

If they have heard <u>BAD</u> things about your company: There is a certain way that you show the prospect this presentation folder, the idea is not to bore them with 10 pages worth of reading, as I'll explain.

Page 2-4: Any awards that the company has won, these will usually be in the form of full-page certificates. The company I used to sell for were not the best at winning awards, so unfortunately I didn't have much to work with. What I did have was a one-page certificate showing the customer feedback rating being 95%, which was conducted by an independent survey company.

This can usually be enough, especially if you pester your sales manager to have the same thing done going back three years, you now have three certificates, which will build upon the other showing the next customer satisfaction rating. This was enough to impress the customer and have them listen to what I had to say.

Awards: Since the beginning of time, human beings have been geared towards achievement, the ego always wants to be satisfied and to be shown in a good light.

Without knowing it, this is why our education system thanks us for years of hard study and work, by presenting us with a piece of paper with some words written on it in a fancy font, sometimes with some colorful decoration too. It still amazes me that the system is so powerful that it has tricked us to work hard for this piece of paper...

But yet people perceive it as something more than a piece of paper, as if it has immense value. The only value this piece of paper has, is the emotional value and the emotional effort that you put into achieving it. I can say this, because most of my salespeople have a University degree, and yet you don't need a degree to be a sales person.

Because of this phenomenon, you can use awards and certificates to your advantage to create huge leverage between where your prospect currently is and where you want them to be. Sometimes the certificate or award doesn't even need to be that impressive.

As mentioned above, the three certificates I would use at my first sales company, simply said that we had a high customer satisfaction rating. The certificate was then made to look extremely elegant and fancy with gold lettering and a thick border with fancy italics as the text, not too dissimilar to the sort of thing a University would give out actually.

The most important thing is to ascertain what your prospect already knows about your company. The following will help you to understand what action to take dependent on the prospects knowledge.

Page 5: Your accreditations and qualifications: use images to show this and don't spend too much time explaining what they all are as the prospect usually isn't that interested as it doesn't help them. It's more to show credibility from your side.

Here's an example for a renewable energy company:

All our Engineers are F-GAS for Refrigeration GAS SAFE for Gas & OFTEC for oil boilers. We supply WORCESTER BOSCH boilers and provide a 8 YEAR Warranty.

Page 6-7: Any press/media the company has received. The last sales company I worked for had a PR department, so I was very fortunate that I had pages worth of positive press to choose from. The thing that surprised me the most, was that I was the only salesperson that was going to the PR department regularly for our latest press clippings, the other sales reps were not using any media or awards as social proof.

If you're in this fortunate situation and you have a plethora of press articles to choose from, it's best to shrink articles down and put several on one page. I would go for the magic number of four per page, again, three pages worth is more than sufficient as this gives you 12 clippings.

Page 8: A single page print out of the benefits of exactly what your product does. If you can't get this onto one page, you don't know your product well enough. As an example, I was selling a very complex heating unit, everyone said we needed six pages to explain how it worked. We had the engineers, management, inventors, PR, and even the marketing and design team in the room. They all agreed that we just couldn't get it onto one page and that it needed six pages, six pages!

This frustrated me to no end, so I went home and created a picture showing how the system worked, then I created images of the different features of the system, such as the digital aspects which were quite unique, followed by a list of all the benefits underneath, and that was it. It all fit on one page quite comfortably and this is what I used for my folder.

Whenever my prospect would ask how the system works, I would show them this single page document as an example, saying that I would go into detail on how the system works later. This would always satisfy the customers' curiosity enough to give me some breathing room to be able to go through my presentation properly. By the end, most customers were not interested how the system worked; they just wanted to know what the benefits were, which I had explained in detail by this point.

Pages 9-12: Testimonials.

The biggest objection I was receiving daily was that the customer didn't know enough about the company or product as it was so new.

The more I thought on this challenge, the more solutions I found. Once I sat down and decided that I wasn't going to leave my seat until I had solved this challenge, I wrote, and wrote for what seemed like hours.

I wrote down all the ways that I could bridge the gap between where the customer WAS, and where I wanted them to BE. I came to realize that confidence is not a 'thing' that can be measured (which was the real challenge here). A 'thing' is a chair or a table, they're fixed. If someone lost confidence in the chair, it would make no difference to the chair, it would still be a chair.

But confidence cannot be quantified in the same way as a physical object because it's an emotion. And once I realized this, the solution was simple.

I asked the question: what gives a product or service a confident perception to the end user? The answer was simply this: **When other people say it's good.** That's it, that's all it comes down to, SOCIAL PROOF. If the community believes something is good, then that product IS good. Once I had come to this realisation, I looked at what creates social proof within the community and I came up with the following:

Testimonials: the more testimonials something has, the higher the perceived quality is of that product. Amazon realised this early on, and that's why they have the five-star rating system for all of their products. Therefore, the more testimonials received, the better the product will sell. Another strange phenomenon to be aware of here, is that even if a product has a number of negative reviews, if the number of positive reviews outweigh the negative by a ratio of 5:1, it's almost as if the negative reviews are irrelevant and are ignored.

This can be demonstrated by the Amazon products who have 100 negative 'one star' reviews, yet because they have 500 positive four or five star reviews (which are probably fake and have been fabricated), this product will sell better than a superior product that has 10 reviews, which are all four and five star. You can use this phenomenon to your advantage by collecting and showing as many testimonials as you possibly can, because how can hundreds of people possibly be wrong?

I would recommend having as many pages of testimonials as you possibly can. Each page should have three or four testimonials, make sure that you print these testimonials in a large font so that people with poor vision can read them clearly. When I was selling, I had so many testimonials that I kept an extra presenter just for all of my customer testimonials. I had hundreds of them.

Eventually, I had the same for all the PR and press clippings too. I would always open these folders and leave them on the table throughout the entire presentation. This allowed my prospects to see that several hundred people were already using the product and were very satisfied with it and even the media were on-board. This is ultimate social proof.

When you first start out, you may not have any customers, therefore you may not have any testimonials that you can print to put in here. In this situation, ask your sales manager for testimonials from across the company. The majority of customers will have never been asked for a testimonial anyway, less than 1% are ever asked for a testimonial.

All you simply do, is call up the customer stating that you are from the customer services department and would like to know their opinion on the product/service. Write down whatever they say to you and at the end of the conversation, ask the customer if they mind if you were to write up just a couple of lines as a testimonial. Make it clear that you will not print any of their personal information; this will ensure that they all say yes to your kind request, especially if they have been very satisfied with the level of service.

Again here's an example of a good testimonial:

'When I had my regional sales managers tell our salespeople that there was a compulsory sales training coming up, you should have heard the whining and moaning, it was like being on the school playground again. After the training, they were still whining and moaning, but this time because we hadn't booked Neil McCoy-Ward for longer than 2 days!'

- John S, National Sales Director.

Pages 13-14: Here you should show two sets of graphs, these graphs should present visual evidence of the benefits of your product. For example, if you are selling something that saves money, you should make a graph demonstrating this. The reason I say to produce two graphs, is because the left graph should represent the past prices, and the right graph should represent the future showing huge cost savings (as an example).

There's an interesting phenomena around graphs in that over 80% of people believe what they see in a graph, no matter how absurd or far out the findings! If you add a logo or piece of text in the bottom corner of the graph showing that the data was collected by an official body, the ratio goes up from 80% to a staggering 95%! For this reason alone, it's important that you add a comment as to how the data was collected.

If you want to, you can also show your prospect your company website, however I very rarely ever recommend this due to having a strict time schedule during appointments. But by showing the company website, you build more credibility as it shows you are a real company with an online presence too.

There is also an argument regarding showing a professionally made company video, again this is something that I don't do and don't teach, purely because of the time aspect. But if you feel that you have enough time to show the company promotional video, and the video is packed full of benefits and credibility as discussed above, then this will only help your case. I certainly have a high energy professional video for my own work.

If you are going to show the website and video, make sure you have this on a digital tablet. There's nothing worse than the salesperson stopping, interrupting the flow of the presentation to pull out a large cumbersome laptop, then spending five minutes trying to get the Internet to work, the website to load and then the video.

If you have it on a tablet, make sure the video is downloaded into your 'saved videos' section so you're not relying on an Internet connection to view it, the same goes for the website.

I want to emphasize here the importance of your presentation folder, because many people will tell you that you don't need one, or that it's not that important. So the first thing to say is that, prior to having and using a presenter, my sales stats were very low.

I tried so many things to increase my conversions, but it seemed as though for all the hours of effort put in, I was only receiving a miniscule amount in terms of improvement. It was only when I stopped to contemplate on how I could increase the confidence in my company and product, that I came up with this idea of creating the presentation folder in this way.

CHAPTER 5, PART 2

At this point you've now assessed the clients biggest challenges, but have not yet started to provide 'direct' solutions.

Your job during this stage is to show your client how the product or service you offer, will solve some or **ALL** of the challenges they mentioned to you at the start of the presentation. Where many salespeople waste the rapport building time making small talk, I recommend you use this time to both build rapport and find out the challenges that your client is currently having. This also shows professionalism, as many busy and important people do not want to make small talk; I certainly don't.

Let's take an example here then from one of the companies I personally own:

You are one of the sales professionals for my unique property management company, you have just been on a lead and your prospect informed you that they have an apartment complex that has a void of 40% of it's 100 apartments (a void means **empty**).

In this case, that means a 40% loss of potential income through 40 empty apartments. For the owner, this is a huge **problem**. For the property management company that I own, this is a huge **opportunity**.

The **challenge** here for the client is the loss of income, the **solution** would be a full complex making the client money.

The client currently has great **pain**, and they want to move from pain into **pleasure**, as do all human beings.

Now let's say that the client tells you they have already gone through several property management companies, who have been unsuccessful in renting the units…

The client now feels dismayed because they have exhausted all options to solve this problem and they are now thinking of selling the complex and investing elsewhere.

However, my company that you work for has a unique offering which the other companies in the marketplace do not have, you have a USP (Unique Selling Proposition), which in the sales profession is a huge advantage.

★★★★★

> ***Top Tip:***
>
> ***You want to make sure that the company you work for has a USP in the marketplace, if they don't have a USP, then they need to be the best in terms of customer service or product (or better yet, both!) When you own a company that has all three (a USP, the best Customer Service & Product) then you are in the best possible position.***

My company has a contract with a large local employer to provide accommodation for their workforce. Because of this, you are able to 'broker' a deal for the entire complex, for which you would charge a premium rate.

This is not the time to discuss rates and prices with the client, even though the client will more than likely ask you at this stage. The reason you do not discuss price at this point, is because this sales system is designed to use human behavioural psychology and universal laws, such as the law of reciprocity.

The more time and consideration you spend on your client's problem, the more indebted they feel to you, and in most cases will pay almost any price (if they can afford it) to have their problem solved.

How you present your product or service at this stage is entirely up to you, however there is a structure to follow, which will allow this stage to flow smoothly. How you do it, is simple:

You take your notes from the beginning of the presentation (which lists the prospects pains.). You then write these pains down on a clean sheet of paper as bullet points and ask your prospect to confirm that these are all the challenges they are having right now (notice I don't use the word 'problems' – because the word problem has a negative connotation in people, hence why you call the problems '<u>challenges</u>`).

Using your product or service, you then start with their biggest pain and describe how your product or service will resolve this pain, thereby giving them greater pleasure.

Let me show you an example of how this will look:

<u>Challenge:</u>

- HUGE Void of 40% losing the prospect £40,000 per month (@£1,000.00 per apartment, per month).
- Apartments falling into disrepair due to not being lived in, costing £50 per unit, (£2,000) per month in maintenance and cleaning.
- Complex still has the same overheads for utility base costs, waste removal and local taxes costing £4,000 per month (£100 per empty apartment).
- Local residents and investors are now seeing the large void, which is driving down the price of the complex and the individual apartments by as much as 1% per month. (Based on a £20M valuation, this drives values down by as much as £200,000 per month on the entire complex!)
- The bank is getting nervous of their initial loan and could be called in at any minute, which could bankrupt your prospect.
- Your prospect is frustrated due to no other agent having been able to resolve this by renting all the units out.

So you see, on the surface of things this seems like a very simple problem, but the more you delve into this challenge, the more complex it becomes and the more pain you find.

In sales, the more pain you can uncover by going deeper, the more problems you can solve.

The more problems you solve for your client, the more money they will be willing to pay you!

Let's look at the solutions now then:

- HUGE Void of 40% losing prospect £40,000 per month (@£1,000.00 per apartment, per month).

Solution: "Our company offer a guaranteed rent program, which means that if the apartment complex is empty, it makes no difference to your income. You still receive the full agreed monthly income." (Notice I haven't said at this stage what amount that will be).

- Apartments falling into disrepair due to not being lived in, costing £50 per unit, (£2,000) per month in maintenance and cleaning.

Solution: "With the guaranteed rent program, this would no longer be a challenge for you as your rent is guaranteed."

- Complex still has the same overheads for utility base costs, waste removal and local taxes costing £4,000 per month (£100 per empty apartment).

Solution: "With the guaranteed rental income, this would now cover these expenses."

- Local residents and investors are now seeing the large

void, which is driving down the price of the complex and the individual apartments by as much as 1% per month.

Solution: "Based on the value of this complex being £20M, this drives the overall value down by as much as £200,000 per month on the entire complex! Are you aware of this?!" - Prospect: "Yes/No/Not sure, etc." – "Once the complex is fully tenanted again, this will increase prices due to a high demand and in the long run, increase the value of the complex again."

- The bank is getting nervous of their initial loan which could be called in at any minute, this could bankrupt the prospect.

Solution: "Once the complex is fully tenanted, the bank would have no reason to call in your loan, meaning that the risk of bankruptcy would have gone away for this particular challenge."

- Frustration as no other agent has been able to resolve this.

Solution: "I'm not going to talk badly about or criticise the other agents you have dealt with, all I will say is that you have my word that our company can take care of this for you as we already have at least one potential client in place and we will broker and manage the entire process from start to finish, this will alleviate your stress. In fact I'll even have a contract drawn up this week so you can take a couple of days off whilst I handle this for you."

Now, if you were the prospect here, would you want to take

this deal? Does it solve every single problem that you're currently having? I would say YES. And this is what sales is all about, it's about finding the prospects pains, and offering them a solution to these pains.

However, most salespeople do not follow this logical process, instead, they will not even consider the prospects current problems. As if a robot on autopilot, they will just present their product regardless of whether it suits the prospects needs or not.

I would say that 80% of the sales professionals do this, which is a staggering number. So just by following this simple principle alone, will put you in the top 20% of sales professionals in the marketplace.

Once you have presented the solutions to the prospects challenges, you have now done the bulk of the work and your prospect will more than likely be in 'buying mode'. But just in case they are not quite there yet, this is where you present your full 'Benefits Stack' to the prospect.

What is it Benefits Stack?

Here's an example of a benefits stack from my property management company that we were just talking about:

> **Property agreement for 3-5 years with Guaranteed Rent** = No risk of void periods ever again (more money in your pocket).
>
> **Only rented to working professionals in full time employment** = Extremely low risk of property damage or tenants not paying the rent to us, and even if they didn't pay, the rent is

still guaranteed for you.

The property has a weekly cleaner = This keeps your property clean and prevents problems such as mold, deterioration of kitchen and carpets, etc.

Minimum wear and tear = We take care of your property for you in such a way that you don't have to worry about wear and tear, we also replace any furniture or items that get damaged.

We take care of small repairs and maintenance issues = More money in your pocket, less time out of your social life dealing with problems. In fact, you won't even know about any issues until you get your annual report showing what we have upgraded or repaired for you, all at our own cost.

We cover the rent guarantee regardless of whether the house is full or not = Complete peace of mind that the money will be coming in every month all under a legally binding contract for you.

We pay all utilities from our own bank account = You don't need to worry about any bills or the tenants not setting up the utility accounts correctly and leaving bills in your name (which we know affects most landlords at some point causing a lot of stress and hassle.)

No more having to deal with problem tenants = Let's be honest, a lot of tenants are difficult, and that's why we don't take in difficult tenants and even if we did, you wouldn't have to deal with them anyway.

No more calls in the middle of the night to deal with serious

issues = The tenants receive a booklet with 24 hour emergency numbers inside, as well as a guide to living in a shared house which explains what to do in an emergency situation. We also have a duty staff member for emergency situations.

If needed we will give your property a light refurbishment = This is done at our own expense.

We will liaise with you to organise larger maintenance issues = We will take care of the normal maintenance issues such as a broken toilet seat, shower head and door off the hinge, etc.

We take care of Deposits & Referencing = All deposits and referencing is done in house by our staff and paid into the Government Deposit program.

Fully managed by our experienced team = We have a fantastic management team, second to none in the City! Our team of staff and trades people have been built up through trial and error over the past decade, we trust our trades people implicitly, they are the BEST and due to the high volume of work we give them, they do the best work for us, for good costs.

We have our own gardener = Our gardener will keep your front and back gardens looking clean and tidy.

We carry out our own regular inspections = We carry out a weekly inspection of each properties' communal areas, as well as a thorough 77 point check every 3 months on the whole house. Any damage that is found is normally repaired within 24 hours unless a new part needs to be ordered.

We are open 7 days a week = We are always available and

someone will always be on the end of the phone should you need to talk to us.

Giving back to the community = Part of the company ethos is to give back to local charities and the community as a whole. Please see our website for more information on this.

As you have probably worked out by now after reading the list, a benefits stack is simply a list of all the benefits that your company's product or service offers to the marketplace.

Many sales professionals know this list so well, that they forget that their prospects don't know this list, and thus, don't even talk about the benefits. This is a simple flaw of human logic and is apparent everywhere in life, not just in the sales process. When we do things every day, these things become second nature to us. This is because our subconscious mind takes over from our conscious mind to free our brain power up to learn other things.

Driving your car is a perfect example of this: have you ever been driving your car and then realised you had been daydreaming for the past few minutes while driving? It was your subconscious mind that kept you on the road.

As sales professionals, we often have to override our subconscious mind and do the things that other people don't. This is why having a printed benefits stack will increase your conversion ratio greatly. You don't need to remember all of the benefits, (although it helps), instead have them typed up on your literature, which you will now present to your prospect.

During this stage, you have now removed all of your prospects pains and replaced them with future pleasure, which in most cases will get you the sale. You have now also added the benefits stack, which details even more benefits that your company, product or service offers. At this point, your prospect will be very keen to do business with you.

At the end of this stage, you want to ask your prospect the qualifying question:

> **"Are you happy that I've answered all of your questions about the product or service and how it will benefit you?"**
>
> **Prospect: "YES"**

You are asking this qualifying question to ensure that you have not missed anything and to clarify that all of their initial problems have been addressed…

CHAPTER 6

SECTION II: SOLUTION

SUB SECTION III: FEEDBACK

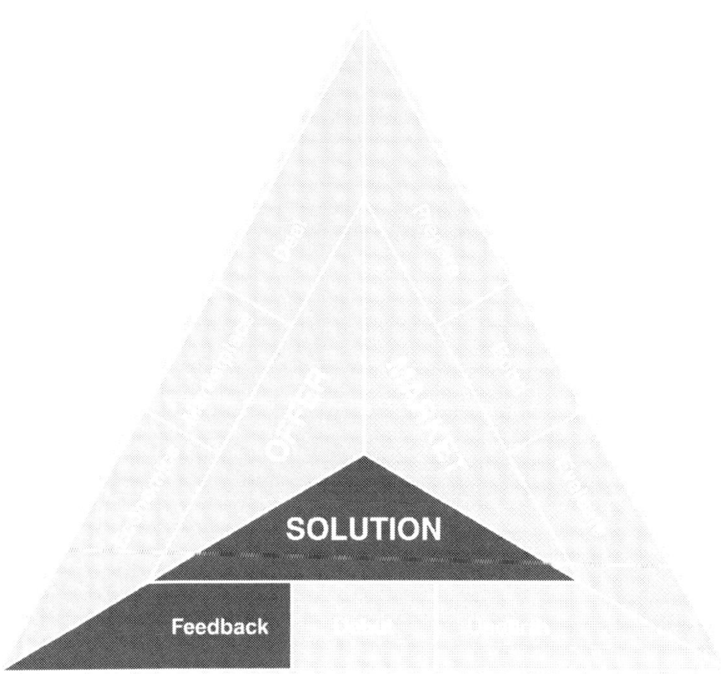

Sales Revolution System™

Having watched several of my sales mentors give a long and detailed sales presentation to a prospect only to receive a negative answer at the end such as: "let me think about it" / "I'm not sure" / "I need to get a second opinion" / "I don't think this is for me" / "NO!"

It prompted me to consider if there was a way to know what my prospects true objection really was in the sales process…

Having read dozens of books looking for the answer and speaking to numerous sales trainers, again without a positive answer… I found the answer in an old book talking about Benjamin Franklin…

When Benjamin Franklin had a problem that he was unable to solve through rational thinking, he would take a sheet of paper and draw a line down the center. On one side he would write 'Reasons For' and on the other side of the line he would write 'Reasons Against'.

Many decades ago, sales trainers picked up on this and would use it to have their prospect write the reasons for going ahead with them and the reasons against. From my understanding, this worked for a period of time but after a while people caught on to the fact that the salesperson was trying to manipulate them and sway their decision. At this point this sales tool fell out of existence and use.

Here's how you can use this tool in a much more powerful way:

The concept is the same, but the language is different and will increase your sales exponentially…

Here's how it works:

Salesperson: "Mr/Mrs Jones, at this stage in the presentation, I always like to ask for **feedback** from you. I've been doing this for some years now and I've found it to greatly benefit me in improving my future presentations..."

(You now turn to a clean piece of paper, and draw a line down the center with a heading either side saying the words 'WHY' and 'WHY NOT')

Salesperson "Firstly then, could you tell me all the things you liked about the company, and the product or service:" (This is said as a statement, not a question).

As your prospect starts to list the things that they liked, you simply write everything they say into the 'WHY' column as bullet points, exactly as they say them. Do not change their words or try to tell them what they mean; simply just write what they are saying as a bullet point, for example:

Mr/Mrs Jones: "Well Neil, I really like how you said that you can guarantee the rent for me for the next 3 to 5 years and it would be paid into my bank account monthly, because this would completely solve all my problems so this is the main benefit for me."

WHY:

- **Guaranteed Rent for 3 to 5 years**
- **Money paid directly into my bank account monthly**
- **No more void periods**

Salesperson: "That's great thank you, what else?"

Mr/Mrs Jones: "you mentioned that you already have a client in place and that you would deal directly with them so I don't have to get involved, this is great because I really can't handle the stress of dealing with this right now."

WHY:

- Guaranteed Rent for 3 to 5 years
- Money paid directly into my bank account monthly
- No more void periods
- **You already have a client in place**
- **You deal directly with the client**
- **Removes stress from my life**

Salesperson: "Thank you. Are there any more benefits that you would receive from using this service?"

Mr/Mrs Jones: "Hmm, let me think… oh yes, you would work with me to refurbish the apartments to a high standard and help fund this, and I can pay these costs back to you over the next year to help with my cash flow. This would also increase the value of the apartments through the refurbishment process and by having all the apartments full would stop the rental price and overall value from dropping."

Salesperson: "Wow, that sounds like quite a great benefit doesn't it?"

★★★★★

WHY:

- Guaranteed Rent for 3 to 5 years
- Money paid directly into my bank account monthly
- No more void periods
- You already have a client in place
- You deal directly with the client
- Removes stress from my life
- **Refurbishment at start, can pay back later**
- **Increase value of all apartments**
- **Stop value of apartments from dropping**
- **Increase rental price of all apartments**
- **Stop price of rental from dropping**

Salesperson: "Okay that's great, we seem to have quite a big list here now, is there anything else you'd like to add that we haven't yet covered?"

Mr/Mrs Jones: "I think we've got most of them now, the biggest thing that comes to mind, is that this will stop me from going bankrupt."

WHY:

- Guaranteed Rent for 3 to 5 years
- Money paid directly into my bank account monthly
- No more void periods
- You already have a client in place
- You deal directly with the client
- Removes stress from my life
- Refurbishment at start, can pay back later
- Increase value of all apartments
- Stop value of apartments from dropping
- **Increase rental price of all apartments**
- **Stop price of rental from dropping**
- **Stop me from going bankrupt**

> Salesperson: "That's great, thank you for sharing all of this with me, it really helps me to make sure I'm serving my customers in the best way possible"

(We now go to the right hand side of the page, the WHY NOT section)

> Salesperson: "Now hypothetically speaking of course, is there any reason that you wouldn't take out this service?" (I say 'hypothetically speaking' to soften the point that I'm now asking them to take out of the service.)

At this point, anything that your prospect says to you will be written down in the right hand column under 'WHY NOT'. The idea here is to only have 1 to 3 points maximum in this column. The one point that will come up 95% of the time is the most obvious, and that's the PRICE.

You do not have to overcome this objection at this point, you only have to overcome this point if they directly ask you what the price is. The easiest way to overcome this is to say: "we will cover the costs in just a few minutes." In almost every case, your prospect will accept this answer, as it would be considered rude to say: "No I want to know right now!"

Oftentimes price will be the only objection, but occasionally you may get one or two more objections, but very rarely more than this. An example of this could be:

> Mr/Mrs Jones: "I'm slightly concerned about who will be living in my apartment and will I have any control over who lives there? Also, how can I guarantee that you will maintain the standards of the apartments like you say?"

This would then be written in the column also, for example:

WHY NOT:

- Price?
- Control over who lives there?
- How can we guarantee the standard of the apartments will stay high?

Always remember that an objection is not a personal attack on you or your service. Many sales professionals lose the sale at this point because they treat the client's question as a personal attack or insult, but this couldn't be further from the truth.

The prospect is merely asking you a question and giving you their concerns, which you wouldn't otherwise have had. They are making these objections in order to find a way forward!

You must see this as a gift, as an advantage that you have over other sales professionals. By using the word 'feedback', combined with the word 'hypothetical' - your client has no reason NOT to tell you the truth, because there is no risk for them. **This is one of the greatest tools that you will ever have in your sales arsenal.**

Next comes the challenge of overcoming these objections. Let's take them one at a time:

PRICE?

We've already established how to overcome this objection, you simply state: "We will cover the costs in a few minutes."

CONTROL OVER WHO LIVES THERE?

"It seems to me that you already have enough stress on your hands with this whole affair, would you really want to get involved with the referencing process as well? Especially as we already include all of this within our fee structure, so you would only be doing our job for us and paying for the privilege, this doesn't seem logical to me.

So to offer some guidance on this process, I can say that we fully reference all of our tenants to make sure they're a good fit, we also take a large deposit and if this wasn't enough, we also ask for a personal guarantor, or a guarantor from the business who employ them. To date, we have only had two problems with tenant's and both of these were resolved within four weeks with full compensation paid to us."

HOW CAN WE GUARANTEE THE STANDARD OF THE APARTMENTS WILL STAY HIGH?

"In terms of offering a guarantee, the guarantee is in effect the legally binding contract that we sign with you. In the contract it states that the condition of the property must be maintained to a good standard and given back to you at the end of the agreement in the same condition in which we started the agreement.

This contract is legally binding under the legal system of this country and would be fully enforceable by any court of law. With this in mind, you really have no risk; in actual fact, it is us that carries the greatest risk here!"

Overcoming objections is simply a case of using your own intuition and wisdom. Many sales professionals struggle here because again, they feel as though they are being attacked and they go into 'fight or flight' mode, which is a reptilian brain response. If you can remain calm and see the objection for what it really is: **a question**, then your mental clarity will be so much greater in answering these questions to your prospects satisfaction.

At this point, you now have everything you need to know in order to complete the sale with your prospect, however as this is no ordinary sales training, we will now go on to add more layers of depth, conviction and subtle closes, so your prospect chooses you over your competition every time.

This will also avoid you getting to the end of your sales presentation and not knowing what your prospects' true objections really are. This is where most sales professionals use hard closing tactics, which in my opinion, are **pointless**.

They are pointless because you have gone through the presentation using logic, emotion and rational thought from a calm, caring and professional demeanor. As soon as you start to use hard closing tactics, you step into the realm of '**Domination**', in effect trying to dominate your prospect.

When someone feels dominated they immediately go into a reptilian brain response, which is to '**Avoid Domination**'. And finally, once they have avoided the domination, the last part of this three-step process is to go into '**Righteousness**', in effect, feeling right about the salesperson being wrong in their attempts to dominate in the first place.

The process is simple:

Domination -> Avoid Domination -> Righteousness.

Needless to say, at this point there will be no sale. And for anyone reading this thinking to themselves 'I've used hard closes before and it worked', you then have to ask the next question; *'did that sale go through the full process or did the customer cancel the order later on?'*

In a high number of cases where hard closing tactics have been used, the prospect has gone on to cancel their order, also known as '**buyers remorse**'. You have now lost the opportunity to ever sell to that person again, and if they tell their friends about you, you would also never be able to sell to their friends or colleagues either.

I say this not based on my own opinion, but on facts and statistics from tens of thousands of sales that I have overseen both as a sales professional, team leader, manager, trainer and consultant.

The great thing about this system; is that it allows you to sell far more effectively than any other sales professional in your area, by simply taking the prospect through a psychological process they will both enjoy and appreciate as opposed to simply 'free-styling` it.

CHAPTER 7

SECTION III: OFFER

SUB SECTION I: ECONOMICS

Sales Revolution System™

I want to start by covering a very important distinction between **Cost** versus **Price** that most sales people never address or even understand.

There is a crucial and key difference between **COST** and **PRICE**.

The price is what you pay there and then, but the cost goes on long into the future…

Here's an example:

> You want to purchase a 4 year old (used) car to replace your existing car, because your existing car has faults that are costing you both in terms of money, lost time and stress through not knowing when it will break down next.

You have two options:

> **Option One:** is to purchase the car from an 'Approved Used' dealership for £10,000, this comes with a two-year manufacturer's warranty including breakdown cover and dealership service stamps.
>
> **Option Two:** is to purchase the car from a private seller for £8,000 with no warranty, breakdown cover or service stamps.

The better deal based solely on PRICE appears to be Option Two, because you save £2,000… And in the first year, that certainly proves to be true.

But let's say that at the start of year Two, the car breaks down and you need to be towed to a local garage to have repairs done to the vehicle, costing a total of £1,000 including the tow charge.

Again, towards the end of year Two, the car breaks down again. This time the repair bill comes to £500.

At the end of the year Two, your car purchase has now cost you £9,500, which is £500 less than the Approved Used car would have cost you, direct from the dealership in the first place. So ok, you're still up by £500.

It's now the end of year Three: During the year you had to spend a further £500 on the car. Year Four, another £500. By Year Five, you hear the bad news that your car requires a £2,500 repair.

You know that the car is now only worth around £3,000 so you decide to sell the car to the highest bidder and it sells for £950. You take a huge financial loss because you did not understand the difference between price and cost.

However, had you bought the approved used car in the first place from the dealership, your vehicle would probably now still be running smoothly as it would have been in the dealer's best interest to fix any long term faults.

Yes, you will have probably had one or two £500 repair bills here and there along the way, but the advantage of buying from the dealership, is that you are buying from the experts. The people who are the professionals in the business with your brand of car.

If you can understand this lesson, you can create your own story based on the product or service that you sell just like

I do for other car companies. If and when the price debate ever comes up, you have this story in your arsenal ready to go. I can honestly say, that when you use this system correctly, your prospect will very rarely ever argue the price as the perceived value of the product or service is just so much higher than the monetary amount being asked for.

We now come on to how to use this step effectively:

The most important thing you can do now is to show your prospect how they can afford to purchase your product or service.

This is the point in the presentation that your prospect has been patiently waiting for. This is where we can now talk numbers and discuss the cost of the product or service...

Most B2C (Business to Customer) direct sales companies deal in cash transactions; by cash I mean a purchase without the use of finance or a loan, often done through a bank transfer. This is also true in many B2B (Business to Business) sales situations, who mainly deal in invoicing.

In my opinion, if you're in the direct sales industry, you always want as many cash transactions as possible as they pay out faster than waiting on finance to pay out, which depending on the industry, can take as long as six months per commission payment. This is certainly true in car sales where you can be waiting for several months on the commission of selling a new car by finance.

If however, you rely on finance for the bulk of your sales, here are some top tips to increase your sales dramatically:

- Many companies can offer a discount where finance is used, in most cases even if the prospect has the cash, they will take out the finance in order to get a better price.
- Using finance can free up your prospects funds for other uses.
- Low rates of finance can often present a better deal for your prospect then them taking money out of their savings accounts (e.g. they receive 1% interest in the savings account but will make 10% savings using your product or service.)
- In certain situations, especially when it comes to money saving purchases, the monthly finance payment can actually be less than the cost saving, meaning that the customer can make a profit from using finance. In effect, the bank is paying for their purchase!

Many people are fearful of taking out finance because they don't want to be tied into contracts that go on for many years. This is actually quite a simple objection to overcome.

Firstly, it's your duty to ensure that you get your customer **the lowest rate of finance possible.** The lower the rate of finance, the less resistance you will have from your prospect.

Secondly, it's important that you study and learn the compounding effect of making overpayments on loans. The results are quite staggering in terms of the sheer speed that a loan can be paid off, and the amount of interest saved when your customer makes small overpayments each month.

Once you understand this yourself, it's highly advisable that you come up with a way to explain this to your customer, as this will alleviate many of their fears around taking out finance.

At this point, we need to use logic in order to have them make a buying decision.

Top Tip:

All people buy with emotion, and justify with logic.

Remember earlier on I mentioned how important it was to use graphs? The graphs are where logic comes in very powerfully.

We will demonstrate this process in the next step, however there is one more important step that we must take before coming to the final price.

This is the market comparison, which we will talk about now.

CHAPTER 8

SECTION III: OFFER

SUB SECTION II: MARKETPLACE

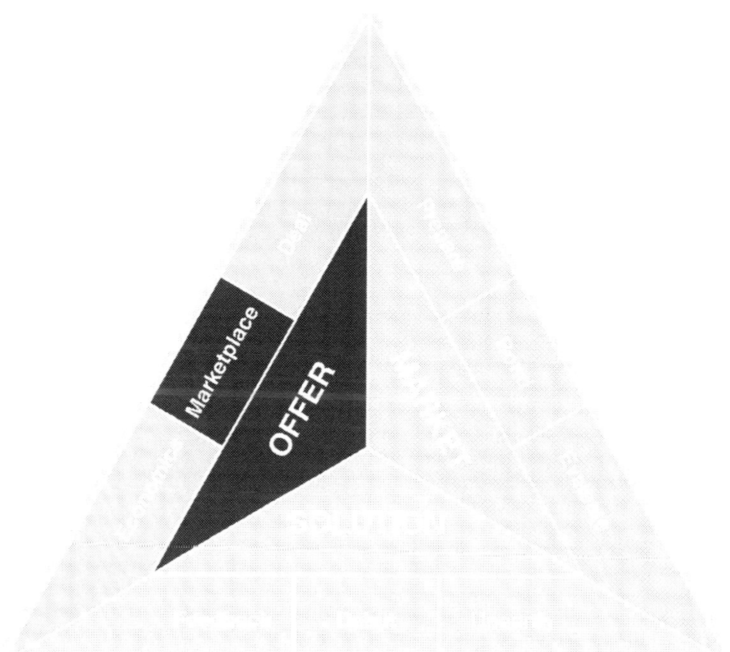

Sales Revolution System™

Stage **Eight** is all about your marketplace. When I added this stage into my sales process, it took me from being the number one salesman in my region, to being one of the top in the UK within my field. I crushed it.

Just by adding this step into your sales process, your conversion rate will increase dramatically; let me explain why:

Regardless of how well you present and how fired up your prospect is to buy from you; there will always be that percentage of people out there, who will want to get two or three quotes (from your competitors) to ensure that they are getting the best deal. This is just a part of the sales process and applies to any industry where you have competition.

In fact, it even applies to an industry where you have no competition. I experienced this first hand when I was selling a unique invention that no other company had. My biggest challenge therefore, was creating a comparison with other energy-saving products in the marketplace.

What the Market Comparison does is to show how great your product or service is in comparison to your competitors, resulting in blowing your competitors out of the water.

The reason you want to print this information as opposed to saying it, is because people will always filter what they hear and make a decision for themselves on whether they believe you or not.

Where print media is concerned, this rule does not apply to anywhere near the same degree. This is because, we have been conditioned since childhood to believe what we read in print. Think back to your school books; was there any doubt in your mind that what you were reading was the truth?

As we got older, and the textbooks became more complex, were we asked to make a decision on the correctness of the information? Again, no.

The same can be said for newspapers or reputable online media sources; we have been conditioned to believe that what we read in the media is factual and true. (Although with the rise of social media and fake news, people are starting to wake up to the truth more and challenging what they hear and read.)

Because of this psychological concept, combined with receiving the same objection each time: ***"I want to get one or two more quotes"***, so I created this market comparison chart, which simply states the benefits that your service offers compared to your competitors.

Obviously, if your competitors have an advantage over you, you would not include this in your own market comparison! So yes, it is biased towards your product and service, but isn't everyone's marketing that they put out? No one ever puts out marketing to show how someone else is better or cheaper, it just wouldn't make sense.

So use this tool to your advantage and you will not only blow your competitors out of the water, but also your fellow salespeople to get you to the number one spot within your company if that's your goal.

Bottom	Middle	Top
(Gas/Oil Heating)	**(Electrical Heating)**	**(Renewable Heating)**
Fuel Cost: Very HIGH!	Fuel Cost: Average	Fuel Cost: **Zero**
Size: Large	Size: X-Large	Size: Large
Planning Permission: **NO**	Planning Permission: YES	Planning Permission: **NO**
Installation Time: 4 days	Installation Time: 3-4 days	Installation Time: **2 days**
Noise Level: Loud (40Db)	Noise Level: Loud (50Db)	Noise Level: Silent **(0 Db)**
Conservation Area: **YES**	Conservation Area: NO	Conservation Area: Maybe
Noise Disturbs neighbours? YES	Noise Disturbs neighbours? YES	Noise Disturbs neighbours? **NO**
FREE Maintenance Contract: NO	FREE Maintenance Contract: NO	FREE Maintenance Contract: **YES**
Annual Maintenance: Average	Annual Maintenance: Average	Annual Maintenance: **Low**
10 Year Guarantee: NO	10 Year Guarantee: NO	10 Year Guarantee: **YES**
FREE Call Out Service: NO	FREE Call Out Service: NO	FREE Call Out Service: **YES**
£7,000 - £10,000 (Complete New System)	£5,000 - £8,000 (Complete New System)	**£ 7,500 (Complete New System)**

Your market comparison should always show three comparable products or services. Two is not enough, and four is too many, because it gives too many options. This is why three is the magic number.

Always place your weakest competitor in column one, followed by the strongest competitor in common two, and finally your product or service in column three. I also recommend using red text for your competitors' disadvantages and green text for your benefits. Again this is psychological based on stopping at traffic lights with a red light and going with the green light.

This entire system has many psychological principles built into it, most of which are outside of the scope of this book but are covered within my advanced training courses.

This is also the point where you show prices for the first time (shown in the bottom of each column.) It's important to show your competitors prices, even if they are cheaper than you. The reason it doesn't matter, is because it's proven that a customer will never spend money on something that they don't want anyway.

This is why the comparison showcases your product or service being head and shoulders above your competition. It causes your prospect to want to buy from you and only you, even if you are more expensive.

People always want to buy the best quality at the lowest price.

You will also notice, that I have priced the product *slightly* higher than it actually sells for, this is a common ploy in sales, as it justifies the price drop you will offer in stage nine.

You see this everywhere from the discount store, to the clothing retailer where the t-shirt has a line scored through ~~£19.99~~ and shows a sale price of £9.99 (even though it was always priced at £9.99!) Even to the car showroom or new house development – there is always a lower price available.

Please note that showing a higher price than the product actually sells for goes against the rules of marketing or advertising standards in some countries, so please do your due diligence to ensure that you are legally compliant.

In my opinion, there is nothing wrong with showing a higher price than you normally sell for if you are 100% sure that the product or service you're offering is exactly what your customer needs and is going to benefit their lives or make their life better in some way. You've going to drop the price for them anyway.

When I used to price my products slightly higher, I would have people agree to that price. Then I would drop the price to the lower price I was looking for in the first place, just to sweeten the deal.

As you reach the end of this marketplace stage, having delivered the slightly higher price, in 9/10 cases the prospect's body language will change at this point. They will sit back, their voice tonality will change from a positive high-energy, to a low-energy tone. This is because, they now think that they cannot afford the product or service and either feel embarrassed or frustrated that the price is above what they can afford or have the authority to approve.

This again is an important part of the process, and although most people feel uncomfortable pricing the product/service slightly higher, it's key. Because this is known as a 'Take-Away'. It's called a takeaway, because you have built up your prospect to having huge desire for your product or service, and you have now pulled the rug from under their feet, so to speak, by pricing them out.

Again, this psychological principle dates back to childhood where you really want something, and your parent or guardian says: "No, you can't have it." Only in this case, no one has said they cannot have it, it is simply a case of affordability or lack of.

Again this feeling does not last long, as in a moment you're going to take them from 0 back up to 100 again! You do this by offering a discount, which makes them feel good about themselves, because they can now own a premium product or service, which is out of their price range and designed for people or businesses of a higher caliber, but for a lower cost. This makes your prospect feel ecstatic and they cannot wait to sign your contract.

At this point, I usually throw in a couple more testimonials here around value exchange, here's an example:

> ***"I attended Neil McCoy-Ward's training recently and to put it quite simply, it was the best investment I've ever made into my own personal development. I took my income from £45,000 per year to over £100,000 within the space of 9 months.***
>
> ***The Return On Investment I received on the training will come back to me a thousand times over and I couldn't be happier with the results. I would recommend Neil's training courses or personal mentoring services to anyone that wants a better life."***
>
> - Murray Alexander, South Kensington, London

CHAPTER 9

SECTION III: OFFER

SUB SECTION III: DEAL

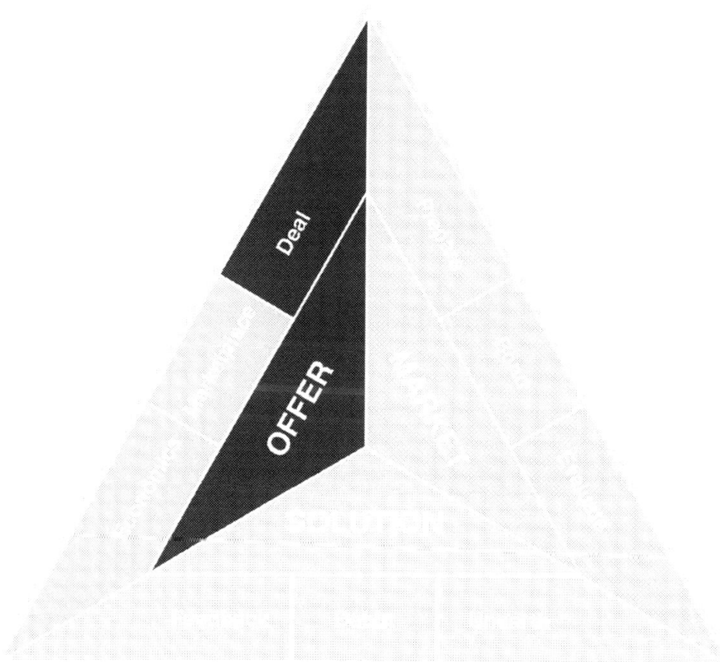

Sales Revolution System™

There is a clear psychological reason why we do not discuss the cost prior to stage 8, this is because the prospect must feel that what you're providing is a tailor-made service for them. If at this point, your offering does not demonstrate a tailor-made product or service, your prospect may feel that you have manipulated them in some way.

So let's discuss how we achieve a positive outcome…

The first concept to understand is that as human beings, we always want to pay the lowest price.

No matter how rich we are, we always want to pay the lowest price for the best quality.

This applies to people with very little money, all the way up to the billionaires of this world who will haggle over the cost of items that cost very little.

The more financially smart the person, the bigger the discount you have to offer if you want to make the sale. However, there is a way to increase the value of your offering without reducing the price. This way you are able to keep the full commission on the sale without jeopardising your income.

How do we do this? '**Value Exchange**'.

My study of **'Value Exchange' dictates that a person will purchase anything if they believe that the value they are receiving is much higher than the price they are paying,** even if they didn't want the item or service in the first place.

Example 1: I was with a friend of mine a while back in

California who loves to buy things from the thrift store (charity shop) despite him being a millionaire several times over! As he was looking over the books, he pointed out to me a bulk load of toy cars that were still sealed in their original packaging from 30 years ago. They were on sale for just $5.00 for the pack.

I instantly opened the eBay App on my phone to find that these cars were worth around $15.00 EACH and there were 30 of the cars in each large pack (there were 2 packs). Doing the math quickly, this came to resale value of $450.00 each pack Or $900.00 for both packs!

Both my friend and I just couldn't resist, the entrepreneurial spirit within us compelled us to buy the cars, and we did!

The funny thing is, that we both still have these packs of cars in our garage at home to this day, the value exchange was just too great to pass up on this deal.

This is what I meant when I said people will often buy something, even if they have no real use for it purely because the value exchange was high enough.

Example 2: If I had £1,000 in my hand right now and it was real legitimate money, and you only had £10, would you trade your money for mine? In every single case, the answer would be yes. There would be nothing to think about, the gain through the value exchange is just too great at 100:1

This time you have £100 in your hand, would you trade this £100 for my £1,000? Again the answer would be yes every time due to the value exchange being greater at 10:1, but this time you would think about it a moment longer.

Next time you have £500 in your hand, would you trade this £500 for my £1,000? Again the answer would be yes due to the value exchange being greater at 2:1. But there would be one significant difference at this point due to the exchange having gone from a ratio of 1:100 to 1:10 to now being 1:2… The next factor that comes into play is **TIME** or **SPEED**.

SPEED is a vital aspect of sales, in fact it's one of the most important aspects. The faster you can have your prospect sign a contract with you, the better. The reason speed is important is because there will usually be other companies also competing for your prospects business, which means it's a race against **TIME**.

As we come closer and closer to the 1:1 ratio, the prospect starts to lose interest in direct proportion to the value exchange. At this point, they feel that they have all the time in the world to make a decision. Primarily because there is no **URGENCY**.

For this reason, I always advise offering promotional rates and campaigns to your prospect in return for making a faster decision, which we will cover in a moment.

To give an example from a 'Heating Engineering' business that I consult for as the sales trainer… this is the value stack I created for them:

Your prospect is a B2C customer, 55 years old, married and spending £2,000 per year on heating their home using oil. They have an old heating system, which is far from efficient. But at the moment, they have no problems with it and he says to you the Old English expression: *"If it ain't broke, don't fix it!"*

★★★★★

You want your prospect to part with £7,500 for a new state of the art heating system. But how do you achieve this?

We would have already covered stages 1 to 6, and he now emotionally wants to buy from us. He just can't justify the £7,500 investment to his wife or himself because he's scared of making a BIG mistake.

1. ROI (RETURN ON INVESTMENT):

"Mr Jones...

- The annual savings that you can achieve by improving the efficiency of your 20-year-old heating system would be a staggering 30%. At 30% on a £2,000 heating bill this equates to £600 per year."
- "Added on top of this, would be the ongoing cost of maintenance that you are currently spending each year."
- "For certain home improvement products, there is also the added benefit of the increasing value of the property 'in some circumstances'. In this instance, this would almost certainly be true because if you decided to sell your home next year with your current 20-year-old system, the new purchaser of the property will most likely ask for a reduction in price in order to upgrade the heating system. Wouldn't you agree with that statement Mr Jones?"

This is how I would propose the close of the sale then:

> "Mr Jones, whether you stay here in this property or move home in the future, you're going to have to spend this money anyway, it's just a choice of how you spend the money." "You can pay the utility company for the fuel, and after 10 years have nothing to show for it except a lower amount in your bank account."

"You can offer the next purchaser of this house a discount to upgrade the system." "Or you can invest this money now yourself, under your own terms, into improving your own home and saving money in the process." "You seem like a smart man, so why don't you tell me what the sensible solution is here."

2. TIME:

At £600 per year combined with the recent fuel price rises (Display a graph showing the rises year on year, let's say it's been 5% per year for this example...)

In year two, the £2,000 heating bill could now be £2,100. This would mean a saving of £630

Year 3: £2,205 = £662
Year 4: £2,315 = £694
Year 5: £2,430 = £730

Potential Combined Savings Over 5 years = £3,316

As you can see from this example, the savings are still not high enough to justify the purchase. In this situation, you just have to look further into the future...

Year 6: £2,552 = £766
Year 7: £2,680 = £804
Year 8: £2,814 = £844
Year 9: £2,955 = £887
Year 10: £3,103 = £931

Potential Combined Savings Over 10 years = £7,548

Now we have rough savings, he can justify the purchase of the new system. When the prospect is presented with these facts and figures, they now have a logical reason to buy from you.

3. EXTRA PRODUCTS/SERVICES:

This section is about adding in extra products or services of a **'Perceived Value'** to the customer. Notice I used the word 'Perceived Value'. What this means in financial terms is usually very, very small to you the company, as you already have the facility in order to offer additional products or services at little cost. But to the prospect, this is often seen as hugely valuable because they do not have the facilities or knowledge that you do.

An example of this (using this same example) could be the following services:

- An annual checkup of your customers system for the next five years' worth £200 per year, which equates to (£1,000) over five years.
- A five-year warranty, extended to ten years completely free of charge (worth £2,000)
- A free energy assessment survey by one of our energy consultants, to ascertain where else you can make energy savings within your property, (worth £500)
- A voltage optimization box being fitted to your property in order to reduce your electricity bill by as much as 10% per year worth £1,000 (Note: these cost around £50 to purchase and 30 minutes to fit by a competent electrician.)

You are looking to offer a product here that costs you very little using your company, but offers exceptional value to the customer.

As you can see from the list above, we have now turned a

£7,500 purchase into a fantastic investment.

Let's see how it now stacks up:

Purchase Price: £7,500
Possible Savings over 10 years: £7,548
Annual System checkup (5 years): £1,000
Five Year extended warranty: £2,000
FREE Energy Assessment: £500
Voltage Optimization: £1,000
TOTAL Package Value: £12,048

We now have a very attractive offering for our prospect to consider… However, it isn't quite enough yet for them to make the purchasing decision on the spot. We now have to offer a **DISCOUNT**.

When it comes to offering discounts, you cannot just drop the price without justification. If you do this, the prospect will think there is something strange going on and they will put their guard up.

Here's how you do it:

You always have to ask your prospect for something in return for the discount. This is called 'The Law of Reciprocity', in this case, we will offer a promotion. A promotion can be anything, but when it comes to home improvements for example, the best type of promotion is something that will benefit the company, such as:

- Can we take 'before and after` pictures for our website and brochures?
- Can we monitor your heating bills over the next five years

to assess just how much you saved during this period?

- Will you give us a one paragraph written testimonial to add to our collection?

Three requests are usually enough. To the prospect, there is absolutely no work involved, so why would they say no? Once they've agreed to these things, you can offer to make a promotional discount on the cost of the system for as much or as little as you like.

In this case, you would never sell the system at £7,500 anyway, the maximum sale price for the system would be around £6,000 for this example (which is already a great price for renewable heating).

In most sales training courses, this is the part where you would learn about 'hard closing' - but here's the thing… if you follow this system correctly, you won't need to do any hard closing. The system does the closing for you all the way through. Your job is really that of a facilitator now, you need to make sure that your prospect has understood everything, and is happy to proceed with the sale.

The only real close you will use is as follows:

> "Ok Mr Jones, do you have any more questions or shall we go ahead and get this order started for you now?"

In **5/10** cases your prospect will say "yes, go ahead and get the order started please."

In **4/10** cases, the prospect will have a few more questions for you here. Again, these are not objections, they are merely questions and once you answer them, your prospect will usually sign your contract and or/give you permission to process the order. If they come up with a reason not to buy, you simply refer back to the WHY & WHY NOT stage here and bring up the objections they mentioned.

If you have overcome all of their objections (which you should have done in order to get this far in the presentation) then there is nothing left in the space other than for them to make the purchase. This is why the WHY & WHY NOT process is just so incredibly powerful, because people don't want to look like liars, they always want to look good.

In **1/10** cases, you will probably have to put in some more work and/or the person may be a time waster. It doesn't matter how experienced you become as a sales person, you will always come across time wasters.

I cannot tell you the amount of time I have sat with a prospect for several hours, spending a huge amount of time with them and delivered a perfect presentation for them to say at the end: "I'm just not interested in buying" – you can go through every reason under the sun and call them out on the fact that they said during your WHY and WHY NOT stage that it was just price that was left, and Mr Prospect, I've shown you how you will get a 1,000,000% ROI on your investment…blah, blah, etc.

It often makes absolutely no difference… In the B2C World, some people are just simply timewasters and have nothing better to do than to listen to sales presentations with absolutely no intention of buying. Don't give this any more energy or thought. Simply forget all about it, keep a positive mental attitude and move on to your next presentation.

★★★★★

There are so many customers out there in the World that it's crazy to dwell on the negatives and get angry about how they 'used you' for your time and expertise and such and such… forget all about it and just move on.

Finally, when completing the sale, always take a small deposit, even if that deposit is just 10% of the total order value or a few hundred pounds, this does something in the brain of the buyer and makes the commitment even stronger to you and the product or service.

Once the sale is agreed, your job is to now make your relationship with your new customer/friend even stronger. I use the word friend, as that's what your new customer now becomes. And like any friendship, it has to be nourished and attended to.

Make sure you have answered absolutely every single possible question that they have in their mind, you don't want to leave any room for doubt or second thoughts. Very often in sales departments that I have been called in to consult for, they have a very high level of what we call 'Buyers Remorse' – this means that a customer changes their mind after the sale has been agreed.

In most sales companies this is around 20%, and my job is to get this down to below 5%, which is fairly straightforward when using this system.

The higher your commission on the sale, the more I would recommend sending a gift to your customer. Even if it's just a box of chocolates, flowers, a bottle of wine, etc… whatever it is they like. If I make a £1,000 commission on a sale, you can be sure that I have a courier deliver a nice gift worth close to £50 once the commission had paid out.

Not only does this make your customer feel happy with their decision, but they will feel indebted to do even more business with you in the future and it's very unlikely that they would ever go to your competitor.

Oh, and guess what else they will give you? Referrals. Always ask for referrals.

CONCLUSION

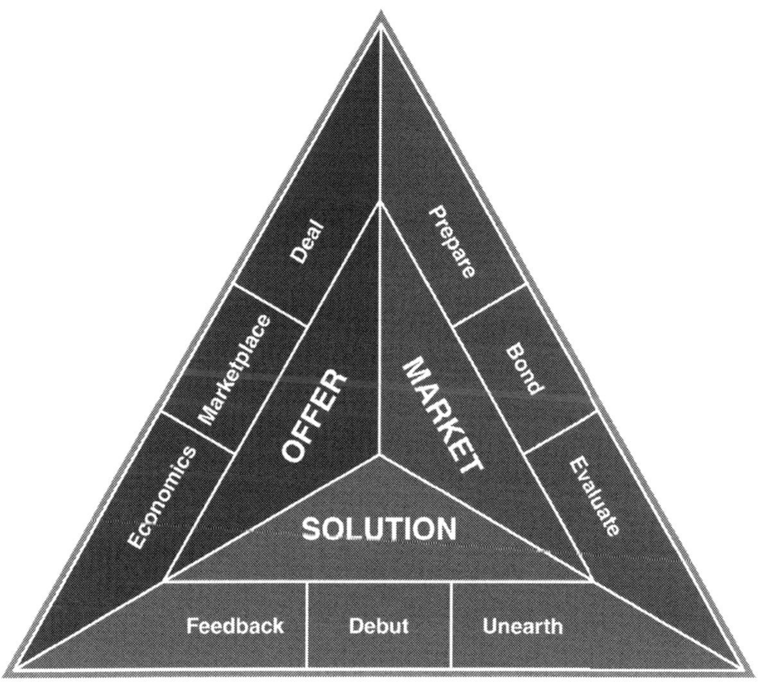

Sales Revolution System™

★★★★★

Ladies and gentlemen, as we come towards the close, I want to say: Well done! I'm always impressed when winners like you make it to the end of a book, because it shows commitment, dedication and discipline; these are all of the traits of a champion sales professional. Added to this... this is not just any book, this is a training course, which makes it even more difficult than simply reading a book because it requires action steps throughout. (I hope you took them all...)

But what now? What will you do with this newfound knowledge? Will you take it and implement it in your own sales presentations, or will you do like most people and having read a book just allow the brain to forget all about the new information?

I hope you adopt the winners mindset and reference this book several times in the next few weeks to build upon your own presentation.

And for those of you that enjoyed this book and found alignment with my style of training, please remember how we can work together in the future...

On my website: **neilmccoyward.com**, I offer several services, including:

- Keynote Speeches (for Conferences)
- Corporate Sales Training (I will come to your workplace and train your sales teams)
- Personal Mentoring (If you feel that you would like to have someone hold you accountable and guide you towards the top 1%, you can join my annual mentoring program – numbers extremely limited)

★★★★★

But the greatest honour you could bestow upon me would be to recommend my sales training services to your boss, your friends or family.

Second to that, would be to leave me a 5-star review on Amazon. A 5-star review really helps me to know personally that you like my work and got value from it. So if you could do that for me, I'd really appreciate it.

So to close, ladies and gentleman…

Always remember that you have a unique gift, and as a sales professional, you can write your own paycheck each month. Nothing is outside of your reach if you just work hard day after day towards the attainment of your goals and dreams.

From one dreamer to another,

Your friend,

Neil McCoy-Ward

29302534R00093

Printed in Great Britain
by Amazon